The Precarious Church

The Precarious Church

Redeeming the Body of Christ

Martyn Percy

CANTERBURY PRESS
Norwich

© Martyn Percy 2023

First published in 2023 by the Canterbury Press Norwich
Editorial office
3rd Floor, Invicta House
108–114 Golden Lane
London EC1Y 0TG, UK
www.canterburypress.co.uk

Canterbury Press is an imprint of Hymns Ancient & Modern Ltd
(a registered charity)

Hymns Ancient & Modern® is a registered trademark of
Hymns Ancient & Modern Ltd
13A Hellesdon Park Road, Norwich,
Norfolk NR6 5DR, UK

Many of the chapters in this book first appeared as blogs on
the website of Modern Church (https://modernchurch.org.uk/).
The publisher is grateful to Modern Church for its permission
to reproduce these, and especially to Joe Priestley for his
assistance in compiling this volume.

All rights reserved. No part of this publication may be reproduced,
stored in a retrieval system, or transmitted,
in any form or by any means, electronic, mechanical,
photocopying or otherwise, without the prior permission of
the publisher, Canterbury Press.

The Author has asserted his right under the Copyright, Designs and
Patents Act 1988 to be identified as the Author of this Work

Scripture quotations are taken from the Revised New Jerusalem Bible,
published and copyright © 2019 by Darton, Longman and Todd Ltd
and Image, a division of Random House, Inc., and used by permission.

British Library Cataloguing in Publication data

A catalogue record for this book is available
from the British Library

978 1-78622-511-5

Typeset by Regent Typesetting
Printed and bound in Great Britain by
CPI Group (UK) Ltd

Contents

Foreword by the Revd Dr Miranda Threlfall-Holmes   ix
Acknowledgements   xii
Preface: Prospects for a Precarious Church   xiv
Introduction: A Progressive Union for a
Precarious Church   xxi

Part 1 Leaps and Bounds

1 The New Politics of Ecclesionomics for the
   Church of England   3
2 The Church of England's Growth Fetish   12
   Reflections for Part 1   21

Part 2 Nuts and Bolts

3 Reflecting on (Another) *Governance Review
   Group Report*   27
4 Authority, Administration and Control: Resisting
   Imposed Governance   34
5 Reflecting on the *Governance Review Group Report*   41
   Reflections for Part 2   51

Part 3 The See of Faith

6 A Critical Commentary on *A Consultation Document: Bishops and Their Ministry Fit for a New Context*   57

7 The Modern Myth of Impartiality: What the BBC and the Church of England Have in Common   64

8 Crown, Constitution and Church: The Contemporary Crisis for English Religion   77

   Reflections for Part 3   89

Part 4 Rickety Religion

9 Issues   97
10 Structures   102
11 Time and Place   109
12 Post-Structuralism   116
13 Post-Structural Values   123
   Reflections for Part 4   130

Part 5 Churches and Cultural Climate-Change Denial

14 Learning from Canute   137
15 Money, Sex and Power   142
16 Forecasting and Futurescapes   146
   Reflections for Part 5   152

Part 6 Respair in a Time of Tumult

17	Respair in a Time of Tumult	159
	Reflections for Part 6	177

Part 7 A Beginner's Guide to Beginning Again

18	Beyond Surviving Church	183
19	Plentiful Redemption	199
20	Coda	208
	Reflections for Part 7	212

Afterword by the Right Revd Dr Peter Selby	218
References and Further Reading	223
Acknowledgements of Sources	226
Index of Names and Subjects	227

Foreword

By the Revd Dr Miranda Threlfall-Holmes

I first met Martyn Percy when he arrived as the new Chaplain of Christ's College Cambridge, where I was an undergraduate just beginning to tentatively explore questions of faith. I couldn't have been more fortunate in having Martyn as a mentor and conversation partner in those crucial years. Faith, it turned out, didn't mean having to leave your intellectual questions at the church door. Martyn and the college chapel community helped introduce me to a faith that not only could tolerate the full weight of academic questioning from the full range of disciplines studied in any modern university, but embraced such questioning and conversation, dancing joyfully with it.

More recently, I have worked with Martyn as a trustee of Modern Church. Modern Church was founded back in the nineteenth century, when the question of the day was very much how modern academic and scientific enquiry could be compatible with a faithful, biblically based Christianity. The presenting issue then was evolution, rather than today's issues of gender, but the debates ran on familiar lines. Modern Church exists to support and promote the view that faith can and should be unafraid of dialogue with, and open to insights from, other disciplines. This was the common view in the early church, which developed its theology in conversation with Greek philosophy, and in the medieval church, which saw no distinction between theology and other fields of enquiry. Paradoxically, then, given its name, Modern Church invites us to rediscover our roots in a Christian worldview that believes that the study of the natural world – meaning everything that is – is, in itself, the study of God.

This, to me, is the real strength of Martyn's work. It is rare to read the work of a modern theologian which draws on such a wide range of references and interlocutors – from theology, but also from history, philosophy, sociology and the sciences. The chapters in this book were mostly first written for and published on the Modern Church blog, and as such they express strong, provocative views on the immediate issues of the day. With any collection of this sort, we lose something in seeing these chapters outside of the immediate context of the other opinion pieces being written at the time. But what we gain in collecting them together in this way is a body of work in which we see Martyn consistently moving beyond the specific circumstances that sparked each chapter, inviting us to think more broadly about the issues raised.

Martyn is one of only a handful of our contemporary theologians and scholars whose impact and reputation has escaped the academy and who is nationally and internationally known. His work has been the subject of a symposium in the USA, and is now a book.[1] In discussing his work in that book, Linda Woodhead says:

> We need the theologian who is well-versed in the tradition but can connect with the Church as it really is. Percy is a 'contextual theologian' or even, perhaps, a 'practical theologian'. With the contextual theologians, Percy believes that context is both important as theological ideas emerge (so even with the Trinity at Nicaea) and for the application of theological ideas in different situations. One of the most striking areas of originality in Martyn's work is his method. He is a latter-day essayist – unusual amongst contemporary academics, but part of a classic tradition. The medium is perfect for his message: the two are inseparable. Martyn does theology,

---

[1] Ian Markham and Joshua Daniels, eds, 2018, *Reasonable Radical? Reading the Writings of Martyn Percy*, Eugene, OR: Pickwick Publications/Wipf & Stock.

sociology and anthropology not from the vantage point of the preacher in the pulpit or the academic in the ivory tower, but from *within* the communities of practice he is addressing – church, society and academy.

Being situated within a community of practice – rather than safely distant from it – and asking challenging questions about it is inevitably a precarious place to be. The Gospel of Luke reminds us that when Jesus gave a challenging talk, he was not only chased out of town but narrowly escaped being thrown off a cliff (Luke 4.29).

The Bible is full of stories of people and nations being called out of a place of comfort and stability, into a precarious existence dependent entirely on God. Precarious-ness does not sound inviting. It does not sound safe. But it may well be what we are called to.

Years ago, soon after becoming a Christian, I took ice skating lessons for a year. I was never very good at it. But one thing that I learned struck me as immensely important for my faith, and it has stayed with me over the years. And that is that you can't skate well by trying to keep balanced, with your feet planted firmly down on the ice. You need to deliberately tip yourself off-balance, onto one of the two edges of the blade, and move. That's been a guiding metaphor for me throughout this journey of faith, and I hear Martyn's call for us to embrace precarious-ness in that context. We need to let go of our clinging on to the comforts of stability, the comforts of the way things were, and be willing to move as the Spirit breathes, trusting ourselves entirely to our dependence on God's grace. 'Don't cling to me', the risen Jesus said to Mary Magdalene (John 20.17). It's a startling call to let go of even the most precious elements of what we've experienced in our faith so far, in order to be free to move where God is calling us to go in the future.

Miranda Threlfall-Holmes
Acting Archdeacon of Liverpool

Acknowledgements

This volume – a follow-up to *The Humble Church: Renewing the Body of Christ* – has to begin with huge thanks to Christine Smith at Canterbury Press for her wise counsel, encouragement and support. It is a pleasure to work with such a gifted publisher who is also a kind, discerning and creative interlocutor. I am full of gratitude for Christine's oversight, skills and gifts.

The personal context for this volume has emerged out of trials and tribulations over the past five years, and I must thank all those who have been so kind, caring and supportive towards me and my wife Emma. In the course of this lengthy ordeal – which at times has felt gruelling – I can only say that we have felt sustained by prayer and love like never before. This care has also been material. We have received several thousand messages, cards and letters of kind support from all over the world, representing not just friendships but also deep connections with the wider world, universities at home and abroad, and people and places near and far. There have been phone calls, flowers, meals, many cakes and reassuring hugs. 'Thank you' does not even begin to express our gratitude. It never can.

I want to especially thank our staff at the Deanery over this time – Kim, Tina, Jess, Rachel and Maggie – who will have welcomed thousands of guests over the years to Christ Church for suppers, receptions, teas, coffees, more coffees, mulled wine ... other events, and more coffee. They have enabled our hospitality. Between them, they have notched up over 65 years of combined service, and we owe them an enormous debt of gratitude for all of their unfailingly professional, cheerful, diligent, resilient and caring service. They have been great co-hosts. Thank you.

ACKNOWLEDGEMENTS

I also want to give thanks for Deborah, Alan, Paul, Matt, Karen, Iain, Erica, Tom, Henry, Jonathan, Linda, Suzanne, Martin, Angela, Robin, William, Carole, Elish, Desmond, Jane, Gilo, Elizabeth, Andrew, Catherine, Sarah, Sean, Rosie, Peter, Graham, Corinne, Colin, Frances, David, Adrian, Nigel, Miles, Janet, Jennifer, Mark, Richard and many others, who for various reasons preferred not to be named.

I also especially want to express gratitude for friends and colleagues representing an extraordinary network of survivors and victims of abuse within the church. Comprised of an unusual compound (15 per cent therapy and mutual support; 15 per cent Comedy Club; and 70 per cent French Resistance: 'I will say this only once ...'), they are exemplars of such care, courage and compassion in the face of their own sufferings and trauma. Yet they have continued to model the most extraordinary resilience and hope to so many in their ongoing campaigns for justice and truth to reform a broken church in a needy world.

Last, but not least, the heart, soul and foundation of this sustaining beloved community has been Emma and our sons, who have had to bear all things; and hope for better. That they have done this with such fierce, determined and persistent love and care is part of the lightness of being that is sometimes hard to even hold, let alone comprehend. Such love, care and support bears testimony to some of the deepest truths that we hold dear in common: that the light shines in the darkness, and the darkness does not comprehend it, nor overcome it. That love, hope, faith and charity are hard to extinguish, and persist in the face of those who only seek their own self-interest. And in all this, I have been mindful – as has Emma – of our enduring bonds of affection and gratitude with the congregations of the cathedral, many colleagues, hundreds of staff and volunteers, students across Oxford and beyond. To say nothing of the thousands of alumni and other supporters who do not dwell anywhere near an 'Oxford bubble'. You will always be in our prayers, and remembered with abiding gratefulness.

Preface

Prospects for a Precarious Church

Whatever mainline denomination you might belong to – I am a hard-wired Anglican – you cannot be a member of that church, or a leader within it, without concerns for the future. Our churches are vulnerable. Perhaps as never before. They are precarious institutions within an increasingly precarious world. That is a world of climate change, intensifying political divisions, growing economic and social disparities, migrants seeking safe refuge, and more besides. Not since the threatened advent of nuclear war have quite so many people on our planet openly said – with genuine fear and justified realism – that we, humanity, may not have much future.

We usually think of someone or something 'precarious' as being in a bad position, or stuck within a situation of risk or danger; of facing daunting hazards or uncertain futures. But the word has a rather richer meaning. It is a legal term, *precare*, dating from the mid-seventeenth century, meaning 'to be held through the favour of another'; 'depending on the good will of others'; and even an 'entreaty' that might be obtained by 'asking for prayer or praying'.

Looked at this way, a precarious church is no bad thing and, in virtually all respects, highly desirable. A kenotic church that empties itself of pride, status and position is precarious, just as Christ's birth, life and ministry were inherently precarious. His kingdom-work drew on the hospitality and kindness of others. Jesus modelled reciprocity and co-dependency. He spoke, but also listened. He gave, but also knew how to receive. He ministered, and yet was entirely open to being helped by the ministry of others.

His miracles and parables speak into the precarious human condition, but they don't suggest we can escape it. God is with us wherever we are: Emmanuel. The church is on the side of the poor. It was not called to make us rich.

In the Land of Exile, in which the church now lives, faith communities are not the occupied territories as some would have us believe, such that the most urgent task is to expel the alien, stranger, invader or settler, returning it to a members-only club. Rather, the church has been steadily displaced, losing its power and privilege in public life over the last three centuries.

And yet the church was always meant to be 'occupied'. That was and is the original calling for the disciples. The church is meant to be as fully occupied with God as it can possibly be: Christ-like, and filled with the Spirit. And, like Jesus, as fully occupied with the pains, needs and concerns of the world, as Christ's own ministry demonstrated.

Our problem as a church today is that we have become pre-occupied with size, reputation, success and survival. Yet God only asks us to look towards Christ and then turn to the world. The church of today looks at itself in the mirror (hoping for some signs of renewed youth, vigour and good looks) and stares in vain, for it is vanity. Our true condition is being covered up with the latest application of ecclesial cosmetics and layer upon layer of missional make-up.

The church has only simple tasks in the twenty-first century, and they are the same tasks it was given in the first century. The church – saving it, or even its survival – recedes as a calling, let alone being any kind of priority. We are not here to recruit more members or followers. We are here to become as much like Jesus as possible, and accept and inhabit whatever flows from that. It might be popularity, but probably won't be (and we shouldn't bank on it anyway). It is likely to be a poor rate of return for unrequited love and service.

The 'truth decay' that many of our church leaders currently

suffer from is a direct result of putting reputation before reality; cosmetic appearance before the crucified Christ; with growth and success elevated above our call to be a people of fearless care, enduring kindness and pastoral authenticity.

When the pursuit of our ecclesial self-image is allowed to displace incarnational integrity, we need prophets, dissenters and activists to return the church to its primary calling. It can only retrieve its identity and faithfulness by looking to Jesus, and then by turning to the world in service and love.

A genuinely precarious church is a precious thing. We need to earn the trust of the world; to learn to depend on the good will and favour of those who are not our followers or members, but nonetheless cherish what we can offer.

An open church is reciprocal, relational and reliable. A closed one is arrogant, self-serving and self-absorbed. If we are trying to secure our future and save ourselves, we will end up saving nobody, and securing nothing, save only our extinction.

No Christian possesses the truth. The truth of Christ possesses us. The irony of our age is that the church may have to, once again, as it did in its infancy, stand for firm-faith-filled dissent, discerning generous orthodoxy, prescient honesty and authentic integrity. Our vocation is to be renewed and so become profoundly, prophetically and progressively pro-Jesus – and against the status quo. The church began like this, in the thin-grey places and some quite dark spaces of the first-century world it dared serve with the love and light of Christ that led the very first Christians. Our calling as the body of Christ in this twenty-first century is nothing less.

But precariousness does also have connotations of threat. Asked to nominate a 'Top Ten Threat List', some would say money, sex and power. Probably leadership too. Others would say not enough young people, too many old people, not enough diversity (that is, ethnicity, gender, sexuality, disability, etc.), or just too few people – full stop. Others might offer a target of missed opportunities and neglected priorities. Perhaps there has not been enough mission and evangelism (whatever is meant by these terms)? Maybe we should have stuck with the Book of

Common Prayer and the King James Bible all along? I mean, at least you knew where you were with them. Or, perhaps we were too slow to get rid of hymn books, choirs and organs, and replace them with contemporary modes of worship? Maybe we should reorganize – merge parishes, increase the number of archdeacons and shut expensive old buildings in favour of easy-to-clean meeting halls?

These ideas all have their place. However, the orthodox Christian answer to the riddle of what is the biggest problem facing the church is 'coping with the overwhelming abundance of God'. The church is a broken vessel. The light gets in and out through the cracks. Accepting it as a broken institution is the first stage in realizing that redemption comes to those who need it. So a church that tries its hardest to be complete, perfect and fully formed is heading for living out a heresy. That body has no need of redeeming. So no need of God. Such insular tribalism reduces God to an idol, around which the holy huddle.

The essays that form the nucleus for this book are essentially an elegy of hope. Yes, I too mourn a church that has lost its direction and seems ill-equipped to face the challenges of our age – which are the ones that concern God. Quite how we have ended up turning Christianity into a self-preservation organization for 'members only' is a subject for another book another time.

The essays in this book – sketches, works-in-progress, trials and tentative (some might say tendentious) essays and short reflections – are focused on the precariousness of church life. I write as an Anglican theologian and priest, ordained for over thirty years (but not counting). I write as an activist for change and reform, not just in the church, but in culture, politics, society and public life. If I thought for a minute that theology was only for churches and faith communities, I'd have become an anthropologist many decades ago.

Precarious bodies, individuals and institutions are interesting to study, because they generally dislike their condition and strive for balance, poise, solidity and security. It is rare to be introduced to a bank, family, marriage or association with the caveat that they are in a precarious state at present. But in truth, the human condition is always precarious, liminal, unpredictable and mysterious. The questions that should consume us are not, 'How shall we avoid this, and remove the risks and alleviate the anxieties we have?', but rather 'How shall we live in this, our age of uncertainty?' As every other age has had its own uncertainties, the question is never about success, or even survival. It is about fidelity – faithfulness to each other, and to God.

This book also arises out of the responses to *The Humble Church: Renewing the Body of Christ* (2021). It clearly lit a fuse, touched a nerve, found its spot, hit home, and more besides. There was a kind of Goldilocks reception: too hot for some; too coldly critical for others; too comforting for others. Some liked it hot. Some preferred the chillier commentary. Some liked the endemic mild warmth that Anglican theology seems to cook up most of the time. It is an ethos thing. I acknowledge it, confess its shortcomings and hope you will forgive me for when it is there, and where it is absent.

No writer is wholly responsible for how a text is received. In *The Precarious Church: Redeeming the Body of Christ*, I have simply aimed to continue the discussions that resulted from the previous book. That said, there are some differences in this volume, and here I mention the three most important.

First, the volume is a partnership with an institution – a dialogue lasting over 30 years for me – with Modern Church. Indeed, much of the material gathered in this book was first conceived of and gestated through their conferences, meetings and website, and here has been birthed into a more public arena. I am honoured and proud to be one of its Vice-Presidents, and the Union has played an important role in my thinking as a foil and prompt for considering how modernity and the church plays out. Most of my frames of reference are also drawn from the Church of England, which serves (at times) as the proverbial 'straw man' in these essays. Readers of other denominations (or none) will, however, recognize that the problems under consideration are commonplace and in no way particular to one branch or twig of the Christian faith. Naturally, this means that some of these essays are sharp, and even punchy. This is not because I necessarily incline to such styling and tactic. It is, rather, a means to an end, and a case of cause and effect. If the emperor really has no clothes, somebody has to say something appropriate. This is often the most obvious thing to call out: 'He's naked!' Not, 'His face looks pale today ... he needs a haircut ... I like his new beard ... nice weather we're having'. Truth, even when very uncomfortable, is usually kinder than the collusion in lies and fictions.

Second, diagnosis and prognosis is essential for any patient seeking to be cured, healed or just helped. Here we are in more demanding territory for the church, because it generally likes to be self-sufficient and, a bit like a College Christian Union, usually opts for self-catering when it comes to faith. This not only applies to the broader riches of other theological traditions often shunned by narrow, defensive versions of faith. It also impacts how that church engages with the wider world. True, there is learning from the world (so we can improve what we do, and validate our practices), and then there is learning from the world (now, what is God saying to us through law, culture and life that judges the church and calls us to repent?). The Holy Spirit – being the least constrained person of the Trinity – operates across borders and boundaries, and the church is usually fairly slow on the uptake here.

Third, the essays in this volume are grouped into seven parts, and as with *The Humble Church* you are invited to graze on the menu. You don't have to try, or even like, all that is set before you. Nor do you have to consume everything. Each part of the menu contains short essays (that is, small plates), written to plead, prompt and promote. I am not expecting any reader to be persuaded by everything on offer. However, I hope that you can engage with the seasoning of reflections drawn from Matthew's version of Jesus' Beatitudes. This serves a number of purposes, including facilitating group discussions and personal reflection. Groups can appoint three or more readers to take a different short essay for each part, and then feed their thoughts into the discussions. That way, the reading and leading of discussion can be shared for each part. In these parts I have (literally) taken some poetic licence and introduced some new Beatitudes to help stir discussion and stimulate further thinking.

In so doing, I have invited the reader to think about the mother-tongue (Aramaic) that Jesus spoke, and how subtly different that might make these Beatitudes if we were to rely less on the English or the Greek. For example, most English translations begin each Beatitude with 'Blessed are …', or even 'Happy are …'. But in Aramaic, the first word of each Beatitude would have been *tubwayhun*, and perhaps better understood as 'ripened' or 'mature'. These Beatitudes have also been lightly 'mashed' and sewn into the book to remind us that there is always some blueprint – a kind of Jesus Manifesto – that addresses the ageless question, 'How shall we live?'

If we are to grapple with the essential and given nature of the church – rickety, precarious, temporary and never fully fit for purpose – then we have some chance of understanding that the hope of the church, and indeed of the gospel, lies not in preserving this mortal, frail body. Rather, the hope of the kingdom of God, and of the gospel, lies in following the preacher from Galilee and his vision for us, society and our collective futures. Redeeming the body of Christ always starts with 'Let go, and let God'. And then 'Come, follow'. May God bless your journey and pilgrimage of faith.

Introduction

A Progressive Union for a Precarious Church

We live in strange times. Who would have thought that Modern Church – founded at the end of the nineteenth century (1898) – would be a champion of progressive orthodoxy in the first decades of the twenty-first century? I might have taken a flutter on the odds. Indeed, I said so in 1998, when the Modern Churchpeople's Union celebrated its centenary, for what was noticeably clear at the end of the twentieth century was as follows.

First, most who identified with the Union were passionate about Jesus and the kingdom of God, but were wary of those (to quote Sidney Carter, the hymn-writer) who claimed the copyright on Christ. Second, the Union had, and continues to have, a strong record of championing social justice. Third, the Union is morally and socially progressive, while also being exponents of theologies that model 'generous orthodoxy'. The Union believes that Christians have greater integrity and authenticity if they can discern the signs of the times, affirming what they should and critiquing that which is contrary to the common good. Those who founded the society in 1898 as the Churchmen's Union for the Advancement of Liberal Religious Thought sought to defend the tolerant 'middle ground' within the Church of England. Back then, the respective wings of Anglo-Catholicism (anti-progressive) and Evangelicalism (anti-rational) were dominant. To some extent, they still are.

However, this new society understood itself as a mediating influence – but not between the competing wings of the church. The Union mediated between tradition and truth, religion and society, faith and reason, church and world. In that sense, the Union was always missional, seeking to explore and explain Christian faith within the modern world.

The Union was also evangelistic. From the outset, it defended the integrity of being a Bible-believing Christian and accepting evolution. Engaging critically with scripture was no longer dissent, let alone heresy. The good news of Christian faith is that it is sufficiently robust and truthful to cope with questions. For that, of course, it was labelled 'liberal'. Some of its explorations and writings did generate significant debate. Indeed, so much so that the Church of England even set up a Doctrine Commission to investigate it, only to produce a report in 1938 vindicating the views expressed. (It is hard to imagine this happening now.) The lazy labelling of decent progressive values as 'liberal' is one of those tricks that the establishment regularly pulls off with disarming ease. The Union promoted the ordination of women from the 1920s. But this was apparently some crazy liberal fad. During the twentieth century the Union was at the forefront of campaigns for contraception, remarriage after divorce, gender equality, civil rights, the abolition of capital punishment, the decriminalization of homosexuality and the consecration of women bishops. Once again, this was supposedly wacky liberals taking over. (Establishment warnings are duly issued. NB: they'll be talking about climate change, migrants and poverty next!)

The irony for the Church of England is that the tables have turned. Most of our Evangelical bishops and the few remaining Anglo-Catholic bishops left spend too much of their time defending the church through endless rebranding, strategizing, PR exercises and reputational management. The public, of course, buys none of this stuff. They are not fooled by the latest sales and marketing patois that drips off the pages of last week's Mission Action Plan.

In contrast, and yes, more irony, you are far more likely to find the Union being the place where the church and world are being urged to turn and face Jesus and the kingdom of God project he practised and proclaimed. Likewise, to turn and face the world, with all its pain and precarious future, or to hear the call for the church to return to being the body of Christ. To be as Jesus, the body language of God, the verb of God made flesh.

Somehow our church leaders can't speak simple truths any more. Simone Weil had something to say about the relationship between truth and tradition, and her words are as cogent as ever:

> For it seemed to me certain, and I still think so today, that one can never wrestle enough with God if one does so out of pure regard for the truth. Christ likes us to prefer truth to him because, before being Christ, he is truth. If one turns aside from him to go toward truth, one will not go far before falling into his arms. (Weil, *Waiting on God*, 1951, p. 74)

Truth is what Jesus draws us to. Truth is all that matters. Truth is Jesus.

There are many good reasons for the Union to continue in its work. The truths and progressive values it espouses are not ones that members chose because they somehow suited them. Eternal values and truths have to be discovered, and once found they hold us to account, for we must serve them. The irony of our age is that those who were, once upon a time, dissenters and non-conformists now comprise much of the leadership within the establishment.

As Aristotle and Aquinas both opined, moral courage is a golden mean between cowardice and rashness. Sometimes it takes a whistle-blower, a disturber of the status quo, or just some bravery and gumption, to speak truth to power. But when that power is vested in watertight socio-political constructions of reality within institutions, some of the structural sin and dysfunctionality that is effectively 'baked in' is far harder to call out.

One of the deepest and subtlest self-deceptions within the exercise of power is that we believe we always act in the interests of others, and have their best interests at the heart of our service. Such selflessness is laudable, but it can quickly turn inwards, with service provision becoming a means of maintaining patrimony and power. A bishop or synod that will not make a decision in order to be fair to all sides may think it is modelling some of the permissive properties of *adiaphora* (good and honest disagreement).

Developed societies are generally aware that one of the major core tenets of political liberalism rests on the understanding that the only means we have for societies to decide upon sound policies, or to make good decisions, is the information and education that grants proportionate airing to all sides of a debate. However, such debate does not leave those same societies in perpetual states of balancing, afraid to make a decision. The whole purpose of deliberation and debate is to decide. We debate slavery, and decide; likewise smoking in public, the compulsory wearing of seatbelts. In such cases, we don't agree to disagree, or 'split the difference'.

When democracies make decisions of this kind, they are invariably based on facts resulting from empirical research. We give little credence to 'alternative facts' in the wearing of seatbelts, or treating smoking indoors as a personal, subjective matter. Facts are partial. Without facts you cannot have truth. Without truth you cannot have trust. Without trust, you cannot have any shared reality, society or democracy. The existential threats to our civilization are found in lies laced with anger and hate. In our uber-power-speeded world of information technology, we must face the fact that lies, half-truths, rumours and spin spread faster than any pandemic. We are afflicted by viral threats to the very foundations and fabric of our social stability.

We are in an age where social media drives increasingly narcissistic campaigns, characterized by a lack of kindness, consequences, empathy and compassion. Narcissism 'others' everyone, then dehumanizes them, and finally destroys them.

We cannot afford to place such a high value on impartiality, such that it sits above facts and truths.

Theologians never begin with a blank page or a pure moment of revelation. Everything theologians have to work with and work on is mediated. This is a central tenet of Christianity: God among us, taking our flesh. Jesus is Jewish, Galilean and Palestinian. He was born and raised in specific times and ministers in diverse places. Jesus is a dweller in occupied territories. He is an educated rabbi.

As Alec Vidler noted, the liberal vocation, faithfully exercised, is both humbling and reconciling. It believes that no party, school of thought or phase of orthodoxy is ever as right as its protagonists presume. For Vidler, Christians had much more in common, in both frailty and strength, and in falsehood and truth, than the makers of political systems and religious sects would usually acknowledge. For Vidler, liberals were called to be free from their own narrow prejudices, generous in judging others and open-minded – especially in the reception of new ideas or proposals for reform. For Vidler, 'liberal' was not the opposite of 'conservative', but simply contrary to being fanatical, bigoted or intransigent: *generous* orthodoxy.

The kind of progressive faith that the Union has modelled and stood for over the course of 125 years recognizes that imperialistic or patronizing approaches to the different faiths and beliefs of others have no part in an authentic liberal mind and heart. That is not because liberals believe that all beliefs are equal. They are not. Liberals are not relativists. Like other liberal religious and political groups, progressive Christians have their reasons for renouncing racism, sexism and anti-Semitism. Authentic liberalism is discriminating, but it is also characterized by a generosity founded on the incomprehensible capaciousness of God, so is pre-programmed to be open to otherness (especially those who are oppressed and denied equality or normativity).

As such, because liberalism is rooted in awe and humility, the humble spirit does not lead to relativity, but rather to deep respect of the other and their inherent equality and value before God. So it can perhaps afford at once to be both confident yet circumspect, definable yet open, certain yet on friendly terms with faithful doubt. In other words, it takes us to a place where we might more readily acknowledge the oft-quoted words from *The Cloud of Unknowing*: 'By love God may be gotten and holden, but by thought and understanding, never.'

We live in strange times. We need this Union more than ever to help keep the church open – to the world, innovation, fresh truths, authentic change and radical reform. And free from narcissism and self-delusion. Open to God too, who even now is beyond the church, beckoning us to welcome the Spirit and become the body of Christ in our age and in the ages to come. No Christian possesses the truth. The truth of Christ possesses us. The irony of our age is that the Union now stands for firm, faith-filled dissent, discerning generous orthodoxy, prescient honesty and authentic integrity. It is profoundly, prophetically and progressively pro-Jesus – and against the status quo. It always was. Long may this continue.

PART I

Leaps and Bounds

I

The New Politics of Ecclesionomics for the Church of England

Your Church Can Grow! Nine outstanding alumni pastors join Dr Robert Schuller for a power-packed Institute for Successful Church Leadership ... You will learn ... how they made their churches grow, what makes success, how obstacles are overcome, ministry principles that work, and how to build a great church ... (Advertisement for Church Growth Conference, *Christianity Today Magazine*, July 1987, p. 62)

I had to pinch myself the other day when reading the *Church Times*. This doesn't happen often – the pinching, I mean. But pinch I did, as I read of plans for 10,000 new lay-led churches by 2030. Moreover, ones that did not need costly buildings, or costly well-trained and theologically literate clergy. As these new lay-led churches will all be headed by the 'right kind' of Christians, there should be no fear of heterodoxy being modelled, or heresy being taught and preached. Orthodox Christianity – the gospel – has presumably never needed egghead theologians or church fathers to guard the truth or correct error. There are many self-appointed purveyors of truth-leading churches in London right now who can keep us all on the straight and narrow. These are the 'right kind' of Christians, so we can all relax.

We were also told we are going to double the number of children and double the number of 'active young disciples' (presumably the passive ones don't count, whoever they are). This breathtaking news comes from the Gregory Centre for

Church Multiplication in London. Many of these churches, we are told, would start small, with only 20 to 30 people meeting in a home. I pinched myself again. Who has a home big enough for ten people, let alone for 20 to 30? Some may, but most won't. Then there is the maths. To grow at the rate of 10,000 by 2030, there will need to be three new church plants per day. That's right. Three a day, 21 per week. The drivers of this initiative are sufficiently savvy to recognize that this 'vision' could be received with some of the weariness and apprehension that might customarily accompany just one more new initiative. Their counsel was instructive here. This is not a new initiative to bolt on to existing programmes, we were told. It is, rather, a reset of the compass. All the things that are currently going on, which are guiding, preoccupying and consuming the energies of the church, can be set aside, and this new, final push, fully embraced, would set us on the right course.

The Great Leap Forward? This seems to be what was on offer, and in a week marking the centenary of the Chinese Communist Party, I wondered at the possible parallels. I had to pinch myself again when I read that the Archbishop of Canterbury had stated in the *Church Times*: 'We don't preach morality – we plant churches; we don't preach (therapeutic) care – we plant churches.' Growth and multiplication, it seemed, had become our apotheosis. Forget care, forget morality: just go forth and multiply.

The article in the *Church Times* (30 June 2021) appeared opposite the announcement that the Methodists had just voted to permit same-sex weddings. As over 90 per cent of the UK's young people affirm same-sex unions and regard such unions as completely normal and a matter of equality, I did wonder what kind of morality and care the Church of England was modelling for our gay and lesbian neighbours. I wondered, too, how we were going to double the number of 'active young disciples', given our toxic record on sexuality and gender. Or address our issues of care for clergy under the heel of the brutalizing Clergy Discipline Measure (CDM) proceedings or being mangled by the machinations of the National Safeguarding Team (NST). Or our care and compassion for the victims of abuse, who are given the proverbial and endless run-around by our reputational PR managers.

I am also doubtful about house churches being the next bright hope for the future. At their last peak, in the 1980s, the house church movement in the UK could perhaps claim a quarter of a million adherents. The number today is probably well under 10,000, with some estimates closer to 5,000. Many of those that were so popular in the last quarter of the twentieth century dissolved when the leaders died, or were subject to intense questions on financial and sexual probity. Many of these house churches would now be classed as case studies in spiritual abuse, the misuse of power, and safeguarding nightmares. I am sure that the Gregory Centre for Church Multiplication has taken all these recent church history lessons on board. But I do wonder who these new 10,000 safeguarding leads in the lay-led congregations are going to be, and who is going to train and supervise them. Bishops, perhaps?

I also wonder if the drivers of this new initiative – a kind of 'ecclesial final solution' – have really done their homework on young people. Even among Evangelical youth, toleration or affirmation of same-sex relationships, people of other faiths and cultural diversity suggests that the old conversionist paradigms are not engaging emerging generations of Evangelicals. Fellowship and worship may be cherished, but the teaching is received on an à-la-carte basis. Few of today's Evangelical youth will read Evangelical books. Many have never heard of the likes of John Stott or Jim Packer. Nor are students getting advice on sexual relationships from the likes of Evangelical gurus such as Joyce Huggett, Lewis Smedes or John White. Christian Unions at our universities and colleges are numerically tiny and primarily exist for comforting fellowship and mutual support.

However, the Gregory Centre for Church Multiplication is here to '[equip] today's churches, planters and pioneers to multiply'. The Centre leads with an encouraging quote from that doyen of the Church Growth Movement, C. Peter Wagner, taken from his *Church Planting for a Greater Harvest* (2010): 'The single most effective evangelistic methodology under heaven is planting new churches.' The question is: exactly what is it that is being multiplied, and why? The bishop and missionary theologian Lesslie Newbigin diagnosed the problem with the Church Growth Movement with these words:

> Modern capitalism has created a world totally different from anything known before. Previous ages have assumed that resources are limited and that economics – housekeeping – is about how to distribute them fairly. Since Adam Smith, we have learned to assume that exponential growth is the basic law of economics and that no limits can be set to it. The result is that increased production has become an end in itself; products are designed to become rapidly obsolete so as to make room for more production; a minority is ceaselessly urged to multiply its wants in order to keep the process going while the majority lacks the basic necessities for existence; and the whole ecosystem upon which human life depends is threatened with destruction. (Newbigin, *Foolishness to the Greeks*, 1986, p. 38)

This might seem sufficient as a critique, in effect framing church-growth thinking within the ecology of capitalism. But Newbigin turns the critique into something altogether more surprising, and here perhaps has in mind the metaphor of the church as the body of Christ (Romans 12.5; 1 Corinthians 12.12–27; Ephesians 3.6 and 5.23; Colossians 1.18 and 1.24):

> Growth is for the sake of growth and is not determined by any overarching social purpose. And that, of course, is an exact account of the phenomenon which, when it occurs in the human body, is called cancer. In the long perspective of history, it would be difficult to deny that the exuberant capitalism of the past 250 years will be diagnosed in the future as a desperately dangerous case of cancer in the body of human society – if indeed this cancer has not been terminal

and there are actually survivors around to make the diagnosis. (Newbigin, 1986, p. 38)

Counting 'members' or the hard, inner core of congregational attendees does not tell the whole story; indeed, it does not even account for the half of it. The mission of the church is a vocation to serve communities, not just to convert individuals into members and grow that body exponentially. Partly for this reason, the insights of Newbigin and other interlocutors may suggest the church-growth merchants perhaps ought to be more cautious when it comes to framing ministerial and missional paradigms and ecclesial life through the lens of growth-success-related moulds. As one writer puts it:

> What is happening to ministries that equip the saints for the work of service when we adopt the language and values of the corporate world and describe ministers as Chief Executive Officers, Heads of Staff, Executive Pastors, Directors of this and that? Why is it that ministers' studies have become offices? [This] may be superficial evidence of the problem ... [but it is what happens] when the values of the corporate world join with the values of the marketplace in the church. (Guder, *Called to Witness*, 2015, p. 37)

Guder's missiological and ecclesial assessment articulates what many critics of the Church Growth Movement have said before. That for all the apparent success, there is an underlying functionalism that may be doing considerable damage to the organic nature of ecclesial polity and its grounded, local life. The apparent success may, in fact, turn out to be a significant betrayal of identity and undermine the actual mission of the church:

> The more the Church is treated as an organization, the more its mission becomes focused on techniques designed to maximize output and productivity. We become obsessed with quantity instead of quality, and where we have a care for

quality, it is only to serve the larger goal of increasing quantity. The Church moves to becoming a managed machine, with its managers judging their performance by growth-related metrics. (Guder, 2015, p. 37)

Yet all the while we continue, at least in the Church of England, to shouts of, 'Growth, growth, growth!' The emerging cognitive dissonance is serious, but we should not be surprised at its appearance in a body now being run as a hegemonic organization, in which rationality and management have come to dominate. The organization, and its workers, have become tools of mechanistic management to maintain and increase production. This new system, to function, requires a constant diet of good news that raises morale and might conceivably increase production.

Jung Chang, in her award-winning *Wild Swans* (2003) – a withering critique of Mao's China and the doomed Great Leap Forward – offers a parable that is a cautionary tale. She writes of a time when telling fantasies to oneself as well as others, and believing them, was practised to an incredible degree. Peasants moved crops from several plots of land to one plot to show Party officials that they had produced a miracle harvest. Similar 'Potemkin fields' were shown off to gullible – or self-blinded – agricultural scientists, reporters, visitors from other regions, and foreigners. Although these crops generally died within a few days because of untimely transplantation and harmful density, the visitors did not know that, or did not want to know.

She continues by explaining that a large part of the population was swept into this confused, crazy world. 'Self-deception while deceiving others' (*zì qī qī rén*) gripped the nation. Many people – including agricultural scientists and senior Party leaders – said they saw these miracles themselves. Those who failed to match other people's fantastic claims began to doubt and blame themselves. Many grass-roots officials and peasants involved in scenes like this did not believe in the ridiculous boasting, but fear of being accused themselves drove them on.

They were carrying out the orders of the Party, and they were safe as long as they followed Mao. The totalitarian system in which they had been immersed had sapped and warped their sense of responsibility and actual reality. Even the doctors would boast about miraculously healing incurable diseases. Jung Chang concludes:

> Trucks used to turn up at our compound carrying grinning peasants coming to report on some fantastic, record-breaking achievement. One day it was a monster cucumber half as long as the truck. Another time it was a tomato carried with difficulty by two children. On another occasion there was a giant pig squeezed into a truck. The peasants claimed they had bred an actual pig this size. The pig was only made of papier-mâché, but as a child I imagined that it was real. Maybe I was confused by the adults around me, who behaved as though all this were true. People had learned to defy reason and to live with acting. (Chang, 2003, p. 194)

Giant papier-mâché vegetables and livestock are not so vastly different from giant papier-mâché representations of churches and revivals. Their purpose is to excite and motivate. In the meantime, any remaining historic remnants of the established institution are subjected to intense bombardment. Their very right to exist is subject to frequent interrogations. Parishes – do we really need them? Let's disinvest in those and set up lots of new initiatives like fresh expressions and cell churches. Expensive established theological colleges and courses? We can train clergy in new ways, cheaply and locally. Do we really need our churches and clergy? We can do all of this with cost-free, lay-led home groups.

In Mao's China, these kinds of initiatives ultimately led to the Communist Party resorting to spouting meaningless slogans that they themselves knew made no sense. As the philosopher Roger Scruton argued, Marxism became so cocooned in what George Orwell once called 'Newspeak' that it could not be refuted:

facts no longer made contact with the theory, which had risen above the facts on clouds of nonsense, rather like a theological system. The point was not to believe the theory, but to repeat it ritualistically and in such a way that both belief and doubt became irrelevant … In this way the concept of truth disappeared from the intellectual landscape, and was replaced by that of power. (Applebaum, *The Iron Curtain*, 2013, p. 494)

Scruton added that once people were unable to distinguish truth from ideological fiction, however, they were also unable to solve or even describe the worsening social and economic problems of the societies they ruled. Put plainly, I don't think we want the church to be run by 'visionary' ecclesiocrats who keep setting hard-pressed clergy and congregations ever-greater numerical and financial targets in a gloomy climate of ecclesionomics.

Like a Maoist culture of old, the Church of England is now being asked to assent to another Great Leap Forward (that is, 'growth, growth, growth …'). In Mao's China (1949–76), it was not good enough to profess to be a good Communist and loyal Chinese citizen. Chinese Communism was turned into a cult of personality followership: to survive and prosper, you had to demonstrate that you were *a loyal disciple* of Mao. Because Communism was simply too broad to police, and China far too diverse to control, Mao set additional tests of orthodoxy to be sure of whom he could really trust. In the end, the only ones left were those who truly followed him: the obeisant. The parallels in the current state of the Church of England are striking.

Hannah Arendt, our foremost scholar of totalitarianism, noted that totalitarianism in power invariably replaces all first-rate talents, regardless of their sympathies, with those crackpots and fools whose lack of intelligence and creativity is still the best guarantee of their loyalty. That is part of the reason why Donald Trump got away with so much. He once said: 'I value loyalty above everything else, more than brains, more than drive and more than energy.'

THE NEW POLITICS OF ECCLESIONOMICS

Trump's exaltation of personal loyalty over expertise is exactly what we see in the Church of England today. Dissent is not tolerated. No voice can be raised in protest. General Synod and Diocesan Synod are primed to emasculate criticism, deflect questions and mute dissent. All bishops are now 'on message', signed up to the Maoist-capitalist vision of the Great Leap Forward with the mixed, fluid economy of the church giving free rein to those with the power and wealth to make the changes they want. This is now our Cultural Revolution in the Church of England: 'Let a thousand flowers bloom.'

2

The Church of England's Growth Fetish

The premise of the Church Growth Movement from the late 1960s to the early 1990s was simple: any enlargement is unquestionably good. Correspondingly, all available resources and thinking are placed at the disposal of such reification, in the wider cause of mission and ministry. Any conversation about proportionality (or obesity) cannot compute. Size matters; biggest is best; increase is indisputably the purpose of the church.

The missiology and ecclesiology of the Church Growth Movement are typically shaped by a cocktail of rational-pragmatic thinking. In the McDonaldization of the church, this is the 'go large' constituency. Thus, any kind of science, engineering, management consultancy, marketing, selling, group dynamics, communications – to name but a few – have an inordinate influence over the theological and spiritual character of the evangelistic programmes and any resources for multiplication. C. Peter Wagner expressed the growth-size world view horizon so typical of the 1980s with remarkable clarity:

> Church growth is that *science* which investigates the planting, multiplication, function and health of Christian churches ... Church growth strives to combine the eternal theological principles of God's Word concerning the expansion of the church with the best insights of contemporary social and behavioural sciences, employing as its initial frame of reference, the foundational work done by Donald McGavran. (see Gibbs, 'The Relevance of Church Growth Principles to

Evangelism', 1981, pp. 227–48; and Wagner, *Your Church Can Grow*, 1976)

Wagner and McGavran's approaches to church growth were, in effect, blended pragmatic tips and insights, spliced together with relatively simplistic and highly partial hermeneutical readings of New Testament approaches to mission. It is functionalist too, which partly explains why the Archbishop can speak of Jesus being trapped in the church, and only met on Sundays when people worship. A missional pneumatology would see this very differently: Jesus outside the church, calling us out. It is we who are trapped. Jesus did not grow churches (or synagogue congregations). He was out and about embodying the kingdom of God. Little of Jesus' ministry led to large, stable followings that developed into congregations. Sometimes, following Jesus – and becoming like him, the body language of God – was repellent to the world and utterly estranged from any kind of popularity and numerical growth. Faithfulness is quite different from success.

Therefore, turning church growth and multiplication into a spiritual and ecclesial fetish is something to be resisted. The church is for fidelity, charity, love, peace, blessing, goodness, kindness, compassion, care and service. In terms of orthodoxy, numerical growth has never been a priority that trumps the body of Christ and being faithful to our calling to love God and love our neighbours. Karl Barth argued in *Church Dogmatics* that it was heterodox to strive for growth. He stated that if the church and its mission is used only as a means for getting larger, the relationship with God will lose its meaning and purpose. Barth reminded his readers that the fruits of our spiritual life are in God's hands.

So why do we have this obsession with growth at all costs, such that care, compassion and morality are now denigrated in support of numerical increase? I think the socio-psychopathology of this among Evangelicals is rooted in fear and anxiety and growing cognitive dissonance. Performance in evangelism and mission is not what it was (but was it ever?). The much-touted stimulants enabling greater evangelistic virility – so many new initiatives over the decades that we have lost count – that we are left with that sense of talk of victory being hollow, inauthentic and probably untrue. An anxiety about size and performance lies at the base of this, and it strikes me as a gendered concern – mostly masculine – that fuels the fretfulness, even though it is garbed in quite different rhetorical clothing.

Yet I sense a deeper pulse in this latest iteration of the Church Growth Movement. For sure, it is Maoism and capitalism spliced together, as one might expect in the early years of the twenty-first century. Indeed, 'let a thousand flowers bloom' might be the new strapline for the Church of England. But growth has become a fetish; a sublimated form of quasi-sexual desire in which gratification is linked to an abnormal degree of craving for a particular object, which in this case is growth for the sake of growth. I detect an emerging 'ecclesierotica' in the body of the church, and this is why excitement and stimulation have become so easily sanctioned as the new 'desiderata'.

The Gregory Centre for Church Multiplication is a kind of Pleasure Palace for those who might gain some semblance of quasi-sensual gratification, even carnality, invested in a rhetoric of fecund numerical growth. The language of 'release', which underpins this, suggests something more in line with what the sociologist Rollo May diagnosed in some forms of self-inflating religion. We are dealing, suggested Rollo May, with 'masturbatory surrogates'. The vision of a teeming, fertile and fluid church is on hand to supplement those who require their ecclesiology to be configured through endless excitements, thrills and stimulation. If you are not excited and stimulated by the thought of 10,000 new lay-led church plants coming over the horizon, you are likely to find yourself narrated as flat and passive in your faith, or perhaps even 'dead'. In this rhetorical bubble, the only valid and vital signs of life are perpetual intimate intensity, passion and exhilaration, leading to growth.

Now, you might be a tad uncomfortable with the appearance of a sexually fecund motif in this discussion. But we would do well to remember that almost 30 years ago, Bishops David Pytches and Brian Skinner co-authored their *New Wineskins* (1993) and argued for new structures and similar kinds of 'release' for the Church of England. Famously, they dubbed the parish system as 'the condom of the Church of England'. They recommended disposing of the parish system – an overused prophylactic, they argued – so that the 'new wineskins' could emerge. (Yes, I realize that what the Gregory Centre is therefore offering are old wineskins, reused.) These new forms of church were based around the principles of 'signs, wonders and church growth' championed by John Wimber, Peter Wagner, David Pytches and their followers, with cell churches dedicated to the multiplication of miracles which, it was asserted, would herald a 'wave' of revival, the like of which had not been seen before. Little of this came to pass. The type of church growth advocated by Wimber, Pytches and Wagner turned out to be self-absorbed with manifestations of eclectic and charismatic power, which led a number of churches down specious rabbit holes such as the Kansas City Prophets and the 'Toronto Blessing'. As then, so now. The church is treated as a passive, slightly past-it bride. But fear not. For if you lie back and think of Jesus, the spiritual romance can be instantly reinvigorated. The spark will return. There will be growth – abundant and fecund – and it will be yours.

I am concerned at this point about the politics of consent. The propagators of this growth talk cannot seem to accept the indifference of the rest of the church – or even a reasoned and critical 'no thanks' – as any kind of legitimate response. The assumption is that no reasonable church or sane Christian could possibly refuse the advances of a suitor with such winning chat-up lines. Surely 'no' means 'maybe', and all they need is more time before you cave in and say 'yes' (with enthusiasm). To be sure, those promoting such advances to the church are well intentioned. Yet I wonder if they have understood the basic rules of attraction, to say nothing of consent, taste and difference. Here, to be frank, many of our churches and Christians are not persuaded by this vision of mechanistic fecundity. In the same way, not everyone enjoys painting by numbers or join-the-dots puzzles.

If we all agreed that the world and the churches could be sorted out and improved by such simplistic diagrammatic approaches to mission and evangelism, we might be persuadable. Just. But most are not converted by such approaches. We suspect such initiatives may be non-consensual in orientation, and possibly even harmful. No one thinks painting by numbers is the same as the art or beauty it purports to represent. The ecclesierotica that emerges in current and previous iterations of the Church Growth Movement is normally found in stories, anecdotes and testimonies. In using the term 'erotica' here, I mean material that is intentionally stimulating and arousing.

Erotica will not usually rely on the face or figure being portrayed as anatomically correct (that is, in art, writing, etc.). Nor will it matter much if the portrayal is realistic, impressionistic or expressionistic. If the work has been erotically conceived, it is generally assumed that the creator viewed the subject matter as praiseworthy. What is then viewed, read or heard will be something to take pleasure in, celebrate, exalt or even glorify. And in this sense, the erotic and the aesthetic will often merge. As all art is interpretive, the erotic as a subject within art is no different. Eroticism represents some form of beauty (albeit in the eye of the beholder) and is intentionally alluring. A lot of our spirituality is erotic – from the Song of Songs to the metaphysical poems of John Donne or Andrew Marvell. But if I am right about the sublimated sexual motifs in church-growth-related rhetoric, I suspect that the type of quasi-erotica we are seeing here is far closer to something more disturbing.

In a nutshell, these represent some of my concerns for the 'vision' of this fecund, passionate virility implied by 10,000 new lay-led churches from the Gregory Centre for Church Multiplication. It has the feel of instant gratification; of crossing the line between slow-burning inspiration and expectation on the one hand, and on the other instant arousal and gratification. And it seems to be promoting a mechanistic blueprint for the church that reduces the body of Christ to matters of size and performance. It objectifies the body of the church to some functioning, fecund parts, and in the process removes their authentic, unique human and social personalities – and their local character and culture – and replaces them with predictable narratives of contrived interactions and instant gratification. The illustrative narratives and testimonies will always have a happy conclusion. The endgame is release and has comparable properties to its secular counterpart.

Gordon Oliver, writing in *Ministry Without Madness* (2012) had this to say:

> This, with major changes in church economics, all leads to a much more 'managerial' culture in relationships between clergy and people and between clergy and those who call and lead them. This in turn leads to reinterpretations of the basic dynamics of ministry practice so that many clergy are coming to see their work, and even their personal spirituality, as an unending series of project management exercises (though they rarely express it explicitly in these terms). This kind of cultural and institutional development is likely to have a strong influence on the way we think and therefore the way we speak about the people we lead and serve. If this 'project management' dynamic of ministry is allowed simply to continue without being subjected to careful theological reflection, it can suck the spiritual guts out of the clergy as well as of the churches they lead. The 'language' of the gospel and the language of those who lead in ministry can become foreign tongues to each other without anybody really noticing that it is happening. (p. 31)

Mao's Great Leap Forward turned out to be a leap in the dark; and then it pitched the nation into a very deep abyss. It plunged China into decades of despair, with internecine competition for diminishing resources, violence between neighbours and villages; with the totalitarian regime resisting external help, and slavish loyalty prized above the wisdom, skills and education that could have gone some way to resolving the problems the nation faced. Researchers, educators and professionals were all annihilated by shrill and ever-louder propaganda. Or just annihilated. As Jung Chang recalls, the people were constantly told that their survival and prosperity lay in their own hands. The people, the laity (Greek: *laos*) – not the politicians or the experts on agriculture, infrastructure, water, health, utilities – would sort this.

Thus, the answer to famine was to preach directly to the people: plant more and eat less. But with no fertilizer available to make the soils productive, the seeds perished. The dearth of agricultural machinery was blamed on the lack of steel. So, somewhat risibly, all households were encouraged to melt down their woks, kettles and kitchenware, and make their own steel. As any engineer will tell you, melting a few tin pots and scraps of metal will not contribute much to the steel production of a nation. Millions starved. All the while, Mao proclaimed 'let a thousand flowers bloom'. The resemblance to '10,000 new lay-led churches' is uncanny. It smacks of the government telling their citizens there is no more money, so fix your own social and community problems. Not enough money to run schools? Get some volunteers in – anyone can teach. People will gladly give their time for free, and ministry can't be any different, can it?

So, the closing words go to the satirist and critic writing under the name of Archdruid Eileen and to the website *The Beaker Folk of Husborne Crawley*. In 'Free from Limiting Factors', the article imagines what it might be like if 10,000 new science laboratories had just been announced by the government.[1] We read the following (3 July 2021):

> The establishment of 10,000 new, non-expert-led laboratories in the next ten years is among the ambitious targets that will be discussed by the Wellcome Trust. It also envisages the doubling of the number of children doing brain surgery by 2030.
>
> The initiative has been christened 'Brilliant' by Professor Branestawm of the Institute of Dodgy Inventions and Group-

think. Professor Branestawm explained how Brilliant would result in a million new scientists, operating from someone's front room:

> Labs led by people who fancy having a go release science from key limiting factors. When you don't need a proper lab, to pay the scientists, and long, costly education for nuclear physicists, then we can release untrained people to just crack on and do stuff with whatever kit they can knock up. In lab-planting, there are no safety standards. I mean, passengers.

Professor Branestawm has been testing this theory by talking to other scientists. There is some work to be done, he admitted, in ensuring nobody actually created dark matter and destroyed Croydon. Many of the 10,000 labs would start small, and some would remain as 20 or 30 self-taught scientists working from someone's front room. Professor Branestawm broke off to appeal for people with enormous front rooms to come forward. But he said the definition of laboratory was 'tight'. There must be at least one drunk bloke who everyone works round, and a spare lab coat and safety glasses in case Boris Johnson pops round. As a mushroom cloud formed over Chipping Pagwell behind him, Professor Branestawm said:

> We must avoid this initiative being seen as 'just another initiative'. Which is why we're calling it a 'vision', which is entirely different. Not the same thing at all. The important thing about this vision is that, when we've stripped talented people out of existing labs to found new labs in people's sheds with no equipment, it's not my fault that the existing labs fail because they've lost key staff, and the new ones explode because Mrs Jones managed to split the atom in the Hoover. No, it's your fault because you didn't believe enough.

Archdruid Eileen is half right. I do believe in Jesus enough, and what he calls us to do. I just don't believe in these preachers who are proclaiming yet another new Great Leap Forward. This is just another costly exercise in our leaders experimenting with the people and gambling resources on another vacuous vision. These are vanity projects. Our leaders will never pay the price for their folly. We will. For our church, I think it is high time for a change of leadership. And to usher in our own quite different Cultural Revolution.

Note

1 See https://cyber-coenobites.blogspot.com/2021/07/free-from-limiting-factors-10000-new.html (accessed 21.10.2022).

Reflections for Part 1

You are the salt of the earth. But if salt loses its taste, what can make it salty again? It is no longer good for anything and can be thrown out to be trampled underfoot.
(Matthew 5.13)

In interpreting this text, most preachers and many Bible commentaries work with a false assumption, that the 'salt' in this text is the white granular chemical we know as sodium chloride, normally found in a condiment set or kitchen cupboard, where its purpose is to add flavour to foods or, occasionally, to act as a purifier or preservative.

Yet the fact that Jesus refers to 'the salt *of the earth*' ought to alert us immediately to another meaning for the text. The 'salt' (*halas*) mentioned in the text is hardly likely to be table salt, since it is a chemical and culinary improbability that sodium chloride will lose its flavour. Any salt that is extracted from food, water or any other substance remains 'salty'; even if it loses its form, it retains its essence, as many a spoilt meal and frustrated chef can bear witness. And why, when 'salt' is mentioned in Luke 14.34, is it to be consigned to the 'manure heap' when it loses its strength?

The clue lies in understanding the 'earth' and the 'salt' that Jesus is talking about. The substance of Jesus' words are 'the salt *of the earth*' (in Greek, *to halas tes ges*), with the word for 'earth' here not referring to the world at all, but rather to soil. In other words, the 'salt' that Jesus is referring to is probably a kind of salt-like material or mineral such as potash or phosphate. These *halas* elements were available in abundance in and around the Dead Sea area of Palestine and were used for fertilizing the land and enriching the manure pile, which was then spread on the land.

The empowering mission of the church, like the salt of Jesus' parable, has a consistency of power. However, that power, enculturated into contexts, does not lead to uniformity. The soil – whatever kind it is – is respected, but also enabled. Different soils become more productive for what they are sustaining and growing. Jesus' salt brings growth and flourishing to all kinds of earth. This salt has always to respect the type of earth in which it is situated. Diverse cultural sensibilities have to be taken into account in the mission of the church. Even when the soil might be inhospitable – rocky, thorny and adversely affected by climatic conditions – the salt is still given. Even where the task of being the salt of the earth is so much more demanding and slow it can still be transformative, given time.

A key to understanding the relationship between church and culture rests on a tension. On the one hand, Christians are to be engaged in the world and influence it, perhaps in ways that are not easily identified as specifically 'Christian'. The power of salt is that it is pervasive and nourishing. On the other hand, Christianity also proclaims God's kingdom – a radically 'other' culture that will sweep away the present order. This is the beacon of light set on a hill: it illuminates the present, but points to a new order. This is the Christ who is above or against culture. The church seeks a kingdom that is to come. But it also strives to work in the world until that time. The church lives between two cultures, and it works for both.

Analysing the reality (clarity), criticizing the present situation of the world and the church (critique), opens us to the question: what alternatives can we propose to overcome the present situation? Many Christian communities at the grassroots level are a living experience of love, care, solidarity and hope. Feast and celebration take place in the midst of the most difficult situations at the family and community level. In present circumstances, the reconciliatory and healing role of the church should be stressed. The church should struggle for reconciliation at different levels, from the personal to the international, securely located in Christologically formed truth and justice. In this mission, the church, following Jesus' ministry, stands with the victims, the poor and the excluded, in order to restore their denied dignity.

This way of understanding the *halas* (salt) of Jesus' metaphor changes the sense of the text significantly. In fact, it completely undermines the most conventional translations and expositions. The 'salt' is not to be kept apart from society, and neither is it to be used as a purifier or as an additive stabilizer. Disciples of Jesus are not to be simply preservers of the good society, and neither are they merely agreeable folk adding flavour to either an amoral or immoral society. More powerfully and positively, true religion, as salt, is a life-bringing force giving itself to an otherwise sterile culture.

Thus, the 'salt' of Jesus' metaphor is a mutating but coherent agent that is both distinct yet diffusive in its self-expenditure. As a result of individuals, communities, values, witness and presence – the *halas* – being literally dug into society, the earth or soil will benefit, and many forms of life can then flourish. Correspondingly, salt that loses its *strength* (rather than its flavour – the Greek word is *moranthe*, literally meaning 'to become foolish', from which the English word 'moron' is derived). Therefore, beating this type of 'salt' into the ground making it into a path is the only thing left for fertilizer that has lost its capacity to nourish the soil, as the biblical text confirms. (Cf. Shillington, 'Salt of the Earth?', 2001. *The New Jerusalem Bible* (1985) is the only modern translation that renders the Greek correctly with 'you are the salt *for* the earth'.)

Thus, the salt of Jesus' metaphor is not only counter-cultural, it enriches 'the earth' and many more things besides, by being spread around and within it. There is an irony here. The 'task' of the salt is not necessarily to maintain its own distinctiveness, but rather to enrich society through diffusiveness. There is a temporal dimension here: what must begin as distinct to be useful ends up being absorbed and lost. Of course, this reading of the metaphor makes sense of Jesus' own self-understanding, which in turn is reflected in his parables, teachings and other activities. So, if the church or the disciples of Jesus are the salt of the earth, they will begin by being a distinct yet essential component within society, but will ultimately fulfil their vocation by engaging self-expenditure.

Discussion

- How does the ministry of your congregation transform the ground of your community?
- What work is being done to renovate and reinvigorate the spaces and places which your church serves?
- In any community, there will be good initiatives that are constantly offered, yet never take root, and produce little for those we hoped to help. What groundwork can be done, so that the seeds planted can become good fruit?

PART 2

'Nuts and Bolts'

3

Reflecting on (Another) *Governance Review Group Report*

Perhaps, like me, you have dipped into the *Governance Review Group Report*[1] with a cocktail of emotions – wariness, déjà vu, impending sense of gloom tipping into despair, a degree of cynicism too ... but also tempered by some hope and optimism. These reactions would all be valid. So, I'll begin by saying what is good about the Governance Review Group, and am pleased to say that unlike *The Green Report* on leadership, there is actually some theology in this document, and what there is of it is appropriate and constructive. However, even at this juncture there is the inevitable chicken-and-egg question. Did the theology come first, and therefore help sire the report? Or did it come after, when the report was mostly written? You would be right to plump for the latter, since, good as the theology is, and it occurs early in the document, it is clearly not the parenting agent in what follows. The theology is a 'Christening' of the organizational makeover, and therefore sits uncomfortably in the text. It is conspicuous in this respect. This raises an obvious prior question: where would you *begin* a report on the current and future shape of governance structures in a church or denomination? There is only one orthodox answer to this question: God. One begins with God-in-Christ and the transforming power of the Holy Spirit. Jesus, the body language of God, the verb of God made flesh. The church as the body of Christ can only be structured once it has realized that its vocation is not self-preservation but lies in life, death, resurrection, risk, service and sacrifice.

Good governance flows from the values and purposes that the institution exists to be and espouses. Institutions that forget these are ungovernable. A report that cannot quite reach for, clarify or identify the values and purposes of a church will always struggle to land in the soul of the body. Such reports are noted (perhaps by General Synod?), filed and quietly forgotten. I suspect that this is the teleology that awaits this latest iteration of ecclesiastical reform. No matter how hard it tries, the work is one of bandaging, patching up and keeping going. Usually, this is all being 'reimagined' too, with 'vision' and 'strategy' as the functional acolytes.

And yet, there are *some* good things in the report: it is a proper curate's egg. There is an attempt to introduce the seven (Nolan) principles of public life, which include integrity, accountability and transparency. Such a pity, then, that the authors qualify their discussion of transparency by stating that 'we have tried to recommend governance structures which offer suitable levels of accountability'. The serpentine caveats, tried, recommend, suitable and levels, all beg questions. Who tries, and how hard? What definition of 'suitable' are we working with? Why are there 'levels' of transparency and accountability? So, Nolan principles almost gain some purchase, only to be hedged and edged out by the people who really know what is best for the church. They are bishops and senior ecclesiocrats. General Synod members, prepare to be reformed; for you will soon be interviewed to see if you are 'appropriate' to be elected.

I imagine that more than half of the Governance Review Group would think such questions were unnecessarily suspicious and subversive. But here is the moment, I suspect, that many members of General Synod will gravitate towards the dissenting end of the Anglican spectrum, for when you start to pick on one sentence, a savvy, critical reader will move through the gears swiftly, from vague discomfort to mounting concern, finally finding their alarm. For example, the report tells us that 'the Church's governance should be designed in order to enable its mission to be fulfilled' (para. 63.) I am sure that the authors of *Governance Review Group Report* do not intend such functional language, but they lack the self-awareness to know this. This is plainly wrong. The governance of any church flows *from* its mission; it is not its cause.

Good governance is but one natural by-product of the church's primary point of identity and only reason for even being a church. There is only one Great Commandment. This is named and identified as such in the Old Testament, and in the Gospels too:

> 'You shall love the Lord your God with all your heart, and with all your soul, and with all your mind. This is the greatest and the first commandment. The second is like it: You shall love your neighbour as yourself.' On these two commandments hang the whole Law, and the Prophets. (Matthew 22.36–40)

The American Episcopalian contextual theologian and writer Urban Terry Holmes III concluded his meditation on Anglican polity with these simple words, which apply to all churches, and to us too:

> All religious questions merge into one query: What shall we do? [Our] course leads to living in the world as God sees the world. We can debate the trivial points, but the vision is largely clear. To love God is to relieve the burden of all who suffer. The rest is a question of tactics. (Holmes III, *What is Anglicanism?*, 1982, p. 95)

The *Governance Review Group Report* is a classic exercise in tactics, but unless one begins with God, the tactics will be ones of aversion and diversion. We see this most clearly in the slight mention of 'safeguarding' (para. 50). Yes, the report rightly says that the Church of England's endeavours in this field, to date, represent 'the most tragic example of the human cost of governance failure that could be imagined'. Here, the tactical trajectory does not go far enough. The Church of England's safeguarding practices are by-products of its governance, lacking transparency, accountability, fairness and justice. Such practices are unfit for purpose, but they most certainly express our core values at present. The work to be done, then, is to challenge those values within the body that found themselves such an easy pied-à-terre in our governance. To be fair to the Bishop of Leeds, who chaired this work, his Introduction ends with these words:

> It is inevitable that some readers of this report will feel that some things are lacking in coverage or perhaps that others are over emphasized. We invite all who read the report to see that what we have set out to do is not to cover every aspect of what will be required in implementing the changes we think are necessary but, rather, to provide the basis upon which we can move to a consideration of the 'nuts and bolts' of change and the legislation required. We invite reading with a generosity of spirit and a willingness to pursue the better governance of the Church for the benefit of all its serves.

Perhaps some slack should be cut. But the problem with dwelling on the 'nuts and bolts' is that we lose sight of the bigger picture and the God who, as the artist and builder, continues to construct this work we only dimly glimpse as the kingdom of God. This is where we come back to discerning what kind of values the text of *Governance Review Group Report* emerges from. Even at a basic 'nuts and bolts' level, 'God' gets a mention eight times, which is an improvement on *The Green Report*, although that document set an unusually low bar. That is slightly less than 'sift' or 'sifting' (people for their suitability for roles and functions), which clocks in at 11 mentions. But the winner of the word count by some distance is the serpentine 'appropriate' or 'appropriately'. Helpfully, we are given few clues as to who will decide upon and determine what is 'appropriate'. I can reveal, exclusively, that if you are enjoying this critique so far, you will not be an 'appropriate' person for any of the key roles as inchoately implied in the report, once this structural shake-up and shake-down has been completed.

To be clear, if you could get the originators of *Governance Review Group Report* on to the analyst's couch, I think it would be interesting. My personal choice for the therapist best placed to treat the patient is Elliott Jaques (1917–2003). Jaques developed the notion of requisite organization from his 'stratified systems theory', running counter to most others in the field of organizational development. He developed the concept of 'social systems as defence against unconscious anxiety', which shed light on the close relationship between organizational task (that is, what people thought the main aim of an organization was, such as production or manufacture) and unconscious group dynamics, and how each can aid or distort the other.

This is the issue for the leadership of the church – the unconscious anxieties the bishops have about success, numbers and mission, and then their displacement activities that try and address their fears. Of course, what is unconscious to them is pretty visible to everyone else, and evidential in diocesan strategies, straplines, absurd mission targets and guilt-inducing, growth-saturated propaganda. The anxieties need to be surfaced and faced, of course. But can the church return to its calling and begin with God?

The theologian Dan Hardy (1930–2007) once famously critiqued an ACCM report on the future of theological training and education. (As the Good Book might say of this genealogy, '… and Lo, CATCM was before ACCM; and ACCM begat ABM; and ABM begat MinDiv; and MinDiv begat BAP …' etc.). Typically, Hardy asked, what do you do with the Church of England's perennial question-itch: 'What does the church require of future candidates for ordained ministry?'

To this, Hardy said, 'Wrong question.' The first question is, 'What does God require?' Such a question produces an answer that won't rest with functional answers to institutional neuroses. The answer will almost certainly be about the eternal values that flow from the heart of God: goodness, kindness, fearless care, hope, compassion, prophecy, contemplation and worship.

Elsewhere, Hardy reflected on the nature of the church: a body he believed to be Christ-like in three ways. First, kenotic: emptied of self-absorption and prepared to abrogate power and position in order to love and serve others, even unto death. Second, abduction: it was to be constantly drawn into and caught up in the purposes of God, and no others. Third, granular: it would result in grains, seeds, fruits, soil and sediment that would bring stability, sustenance and order to life, to the glory and praise of God. Good governance would be a fruit but is not a seed. The Christian faith, and its reification in the form of congregations, denominations and churches, teaches us that ecclesiology itself is a kind of social theory that owes its life and identity to Christ: the true vine. We are but a branch. We are not the vine – just the vessel through which the life of God flows to give fruit to the world.

Churches are not our property. We are only custodians and tenants, not the owners. We do not own the truth. It owns us. Our churches are sacred spaces. But they are also a public space. Churches are, first and foremost, a vision of social polity – how to live together as people, rather than simply setting out the proposed terms and conditions for the membership of a clearly delineated sacred society.

Evelyn Underhill, writing to Archbishop Lang on the eve of the 1930 Lambeth Conference, reminded him that the world was not especially hungry for what the church was immediately preoccupied with. Underhill put it sharply in her letter: 'May it please your Grace ... I desire to humbly suggest that the interesting thing about religion is God; and the people are hungry for God.' Bishops need to be able to feed us, not manage us. Bishops in their oversight should really function as public apologists, in the public square, when they defend the foolishness of the cross and the truth of the gospel, and so facilitate and enable lived corporate demonstrations of faith's endurance – and of the love, forgiveness and communion that is to be found in Christ. The primary calling for our bishops is to mediate the wisdom and compassion of God: to be genuinely good teachers and pastors, after the example of Christ himself, no less. Being a bishop is not an ecclesiastical 'job'. It is, rather, an 'occupation'. Bishops are to be occupied with God (for which they need theology and spirituality); and then to be occupied with what they think might preoccupy God's heart and mind – the cares and concerns Christ has for our broken world and its needy people (and so engage in pastoral care). Thus occupied, a bishop might then be said to be doing the 'job' the church believed and discerned that they were called to do.

So, if our post-social, post-truth and post-religious age is to be addressed, spiritual courage, prescient wisdom and public theology are needed – if the churches are to remain resilient, and Christianity to survive as an agent of social capital in the service of humanity. Alas, the *Governance Review Group Report*, by not beginning with God, landed nowhere near enabling us to understand the church as body language of God, or the verb of God made flesh.

Note

1 The GRG reported on 14 September 2021. See also GS 2249, and www.churchofengland.org/sites/default/files/2021-09/Governance%20Review%20Group%20Report%20FOR%20PUBLICATION.pdf.

4

Authority, Administration and Control: Resisting Imposed Governance

Nuts and bolts have a history. Something like these were used in the Hanging Gardens of Babylon, apparently. Jacques Besson, a French inventor, created the bolt and screw manufacturing machine in 1568, and also made a screw-cutting plate for use with lathes. This was later perfected and manufactured by an English company, Hindley of York. In the eighteenth century, clockmakers were the principal users of nuts and bolts. But it was not until 1841 that Joseph Whitworth, a British toolmaker, and his American counterpart, William Sellers, had proposed a standardized thread system. It was the English metallurgist Sir Henry Bessemer (from 1856 to 1876) who produced the very first cheap mild steel in massive quantities.

Most key policy areas in the church today are governed not by theological leadership and vision but by management. True, in some ways leadership is a process similar to management. Leadership entails working with people; so does management. Leadership is concerned with effective goal accomplishment; so is management. But whereas the study of leadership can be traced back to Aristotle and Plato, management science only emerged around the turn of the twentieth century with the advent of advanced industrialized society. Management was created as a means of reducing chaos in organizations, to make them run more efficiently and effectively.

The primary functions of management – identified by Henri Fayol (1916) – were planning, organizing, staffing and controlling. These functions are still representative of management, and they lie behind the *Governance Review Group Report*. Fayol worked for one of the largest producers of iron and steel in France. He became its managing director in 1888, when the mine company employed over 10,000 people. Fayol realized that the goal of management was to serve processes that produced predictable results. We make round pegs to fit round holes, square for square. Management eliminates rough edges. Any creative friction tolerated will have to be subordinate to the processes and their goals. So, management will not have a vision for an organic institution, where the wrong shapes might eventually meld together, or even ultimately make something better. As with management, so with the church, perhaps? The church, as a form of social polity, was always meant to be for others. Like God, Christ and the Holy Spirit, 'church' is not yours or mine. It is for all and belongs to all. It is a shared enterprise, built on profound notions of charity, reciprocity, giving, receiving and grace and the common good. It is an organic body, not a machine comprising nuts and bolts. The organic motifs the New Testament attaches to concepts of the church are no accident. Bodies with bolts attached only summon images of Frankenstein's monster.

While lecturing at the Said Business School at the University of Oxford, I would often ask students: 'What is the oldest constitution in the world that people still live by today?' Given that this module is about governance and leadership, students were intrigued. Many assumed that the answer might be British, the mother of all parliaments, and all that. Some braver souls suggest Iceland – that is the world's parliament, formed in AD 930 – the *Althing*. But no, it is not that either. The answer is the Rule of Benedict, written around 540. So yes, Catholic, European and designed to regulate life and how we live together.

Benedict's Rule begins with a simple word – 'hearken' or 'listen' – and goes on to tell us that if we want to lead a body or a group, we must first of all listen to it. It advocates charity, compassion, grace, hospitality, hope, holiness. It preaches regard and respect for neighbours and for the poor. It tells us how to live together despite our differences. The essay I then set on the basis of this was straightforward: 'Write a book review on a text that teaches us about leadership.' But there was a catch: you could only write a review of a book that has been in continuous print for at least 300 years. This cut out a great deal of modern dross at a stroke: those tiresome books at airport bookshops that brashly claim to be the latest fad and breakthrough in leadership studies or management theory. They were all barred from this exercise. So, what could you write on in response to this question? Perhaps Machiavelli's *The Prince*, or Shakespearean tragedies such as *Lear* or *Macbeth*, which have plenty to say on leadership. As well as Benedict's Rule, there is also Gregory's *Pastoral Rule*, the textbook on how to be a bishop, translated by Alfred the Great, which is mostly unknown to and unread by bishops today.

Elliott Jaques, in his *A General Theory of Bureaucracy* (1976), argued that churches were an 'association', and clergy 'members' not its employees. He argued that once clergy come to be regarded as employees in a manager–subordinate relationship, congregations become customers and the sacred bond between laity and clergy becomes broken and turned into one of consumer–provider. Jaques specifically praised those churches that promoted life tenure for clergy, because it guarded against centralized managerial interference and protected the deep communal and personal ethos of the clergy–laity bond. Overt central control and monitoring by churches, argued Jaques, slowly destroyed local spiritual life, because the clergy would be subject to demands on two fronts: namely, those targets and priorities set remotely by central management, and the local consumerist demands of congregations. The combination would erode public–pastoral ministry to the whole parish, with the clergy becoming demoralized and alienated.

In her prescient book *The Precarious Organization: Sociological Explorations of the Church's Mission and Structure* (1976), the Dutch ecclesiologist Mady Thung suggests that national churches in northern Europe have come under increasing pressure in the post-war years to become 'organizations': 'nervous activity and hectic programmes ... constantly try to engage' members in an attempt to reach 'non-members'. She contrasts the 'organizational' model and its frenetic activism with the 'institutional' model of the church – the latter offering, instead, contemplative, aesthetic and liturgical frameworks that take longer to grow and are often latent for significant periods of time, but, she argues, may be more culturally resilient and conducive than an activist-organizational model. There is an irony in this. The church is clearly trying to become organized and act like a good organization in the modern world. Its problem is that it is largely a voluntary association, run by volunteers, who are under few obligations to abide by rules, regulations and codes of compliance. Or the volunteers may simply lack the will and desire to be organized. Or the voluntary codes are simply inadequate when tested for robustness. Moreover, the churches have depleting resources, and the greater the demand for standardized forms of organization becomes, the more the churches are likely to fail and default on basic minimum standards of compliance.

So the churches find themselves increasingly failing as organizations but are unable to recover their identities as public utilities and value-based institutions. Their authority is undermined as a consequence. In terms of bureaucracy, we can express the matter succinctly:

> Any social order is a tissue of authorities. In contemporary society these authorities range from the mild and provident authority of a mother over her infant to the absolute, unconditional, and imprescriptible authority of the national state. Some system or pattern of authority is involved in any continuing social aggregate. The moment two or more persons find themselves in a relationship that involves, in whatever degree of informality or formality, the distribution of responsibilities, duties, needs, privileges, and rewards, a pattern of authority is present. (Nisbet, *The Social Bond*, 1970, p. 113)

Thus, social expectations of what it means to be 'public' may now be at such variance with where the churches are that the authority and identity of the churches are undermined by their failure to be well organized, and the institution to be recognizably compliant, transparent and accountable. (NB: the word 'public' gets more than a dozen mentions in the report, but over half refer to the anxiety of how the church appears, and none to the church listening to the public or being a public body.) In the midst of such a defensive response, we are too willing to defer to the power of bishops and their alleged capacity to organize and lead. I don't think we want any more from our bishops than exemplary care, teaching, compassion and goodness.

However, congregations perhaps trust this assumption far more than is really wise. In the absence of arguments and evidence from episcopal lips, assurances and assertions from bishops often carry too much weight. Many assume bishops to be almost omniscient. Yet there must be significant doubts about their competencies in areas in which they have had little, if any, professional training. Bishops, because they are bishops, often retain positions of 'oversight' in fields they simply do not comprehend, such as education, safeguarding and public policy. They often feel the need to defend their comprehensiveness and role in such oversight, even when it is manifestly the case that they are out of their depth, or sometimes plain wrong.

All too often, exposure of any weakness, failure or wrongdoing is met with defensive assertions and reassertions. They can sometimes keep digging themselves deeper into the very holes they inadvertently created. We see this very clearly on issues of gender and sexuality, and latent in ethnicity and disability. The bishops are committed to tepid polities and theologies of equality, so the very people who are sexist, racist or homophobic are given platforms, preference and equality. But the church – and the Bible – while teaching that all are of equal value, espouses theologies and polities of liberation, not equality.

Slaves, Greeks and women who belonged to the early church

were *not* accommodated on condition that they accepted their inequality and therefore oppression. They were equally loved by God, and so equal as Jesus' followers, and equal as citizens of heaven. The radical adjustments had to be made by those who had power and privileges. They had to see their social subordinates as set free: liberated. So, while the bishops wrestle with how to keep everything levelled down and equal, the voices of protest and liberation are not suffocated. To be clear, feminism began not as a movement for equality but as one of freedom. The truth sets us free; it does not exist to makes us bound to stifling equality.

Yet the church is a sacred space, but also a public space; it is not a private sect. Ceding power and authority to wider society and to regulators and overseers with appropriate competencies would represent a significant shift in ecclesial polity. It would require the giving away of power in order to protect ecclesial authority in the areas that matter, including mission, ministry, doctrine and pastoral care. Where the church is ministering in public ways, it must learn to accept new standards in public life, and the authority of these. If the churches try and evade their responsibility here, they will lose their authority. Considering this, can the Church of England now be reimagined all over again and streamlined into being some lean, on-message organization, efficiently run? I doubt it. If diversity of belief and practice in the church could be so easily managed, we might have expected the New Testament to say so. It doesn't.

It is the vanity of our age to suppose the church is just like an organization in which diversity can be smoothed over; the faithful warily kettled into some false compliance manufactured by its leaders; difficulties managed and controlled; and the church pasteurized so as to become a body of utterly consistent clarity. If all our churches are now merely for a small, dwindling group of activist members who simply want to go on perpetual recruitment drives, then congregations and Christian faith will further deteriorate. What we need now – through prescient public theology – is some serious conversation and debate about how our churches can reclaim their identity as proper public forms of social polity. There is another concept of the church to rediscover and reinhabit here. It is nothing less than the church finding itself as, what Dan Hardy once described, 'the social-transcendent', and, even more daringly, reimagining churches as the 'social skin' of the world.

For the promise of the *Governance Review Group Report*, I hope it will be noted by General Synod, and then indefinitely shelved. If God is truly the first cause of the church, and gives us the values from which all mission, governance and good structures flow, then we will quietly forget this report. For we will have remembered what we lost along the way. God matters. First and last. Jesus sets an example of fearless care and reckless love. The Holy Spirit leads us into all truth. We are on Jesus' journey, not ours. From this, we might discover why we were created and redeemed, what we are here for and are meant to do with this treasure within these cracked earthenware pots.

Christ's life and ministry is how the church is called to be an incorporative body that expresses the life of the kingdom of heaven, which is ultimately reconciling all things to God. To paraphrase Bishop John Robinson (1919–83), the church was only ever meant to be the constructor's hut on God's building site, which is the world. Christians today assume all too easily that God's primary concern lies with the church. But God is building a kingdom in the world – a prophetic polity rooted in superabundant justice, liberation and compassion. Our churches are merely 'transitory temples' to achieve these ends. Churches are not God's final goal. They are simply a means to God's own ends. It is surely time to reclaim the priority of God's polity in our governance and the mission and ministries of our churches. To borrow the most-used word from the *Governance Review Group Report*, that would be 'appropriate'.

5

Reflecting on the *Governance Review Group Report*

It is rare to write a follow-up article in the wake of comments made on social media. However, I have made an exception to this rule. Given the careful attention paid by commentators in their critiques, there was more to say by way of conclusion. Readers of the two earlier pieces will recall the attention drawn to the overuse of 'appropriate' as a qualifying term for all the persons and systems that await overhaul – well over 30 mentions. 'God', as we noted, barely got a look-in, with only eight. So I was grateful for this comment on *Thinking Anglicans* that said:

> extending Percy's excellent textual analysis as some measure of a document, I see within the Governance Review Group Report dated July 2021 the following occurrences: Bishop, 138; Board, 119; Committee, 73; Diocese/an, 26; Clergy, 19; Staff, 17; Parish, 13; Priest, 3; Rector, 2 (both within director); Vicar, 0; Incumbent, 0; Pastoral care, 4; Preaching, 1; Pension, 31; Child/ren, 2 (one in relation to IICSA); Govern, 331; Lead, 55; Manage, 48; Investment, 42; Strategy/ic, 36; Vision, 35 (incl. one division); Lessons Learned, 3; Gospel, 2; Jesus, 1.

In a sense, these words and numbers tell their own story. If I were to generate a word-cloud illustration, Jesus would be the size of a small, lonely ant, while the behemoth of Govern-Board-Manage-Committee-Lead-Strategy would be the largest-known dinosaur ever to have roamed the planet. How did we arrive at another report in the Church of England where our 'core business' – care, compassion, service, worship, integrity, virtue, eternal values, kingdom building and community – hardly merits a mention? To say nothing of an ever-shy (but I'm thinking perhaps shifty?) tendency to keep God, Jesus and the Holy Spirit out of this as much as possible. I thought, following the parable of the tenants (Matthew 21.28–46; Mark 12.1–12; Luke 20.9–19), all the church could ever claim was to be managing God's business. It is not our vineyard. Not our fruit. Not our kingdom. We are here to work the land and help with the harvest. As I read the *Governance Review Group Report* again, I was tempted to adapt a John Cleese quote in one famous episode of *Fawlty Towers*: 'Whatever you do, don't mention God! I did once, but I think I got away with it.'

As I noted in previous articles, the theology contained in the *Governance Review Group Report* felt like an afterthought, or just some gloss. It does now appear that those drafted in to provide the theological guidance either drifted off or resigned before the end of the process. They are named and thanked in the report as though they were there from the beginning through to the end of the process. This seems unlikely, and the incorporation of their names is another reason to doubt the provenance of this report. The theologians who it is claimed were consulted are stellar. But no one who is theologically literate can see much evidence of them really turning up. Any report of this kind ought to start with some fundamental questions. These might include, 'Who is Jesus Christ for us today?'; 'What does the Lord require?'; 'What is the greatest commandment?'; 'How is God at work in the kingdom beyond the church?'; 'Where does the Holy Spirit lead us in the light of that?'; and, 'What should the church be in the light of the God who is always beyond us?' These would do for starters, but you can doubtless think of others.

The reason the *Governance Review Group Report* is so poor is that it won't engage with the obvious questions. If you asked those questions, you might end up with some rich ideas and answers about the nature of God and the nature of the church, and their relationship, and therefore the texture of reform that is required. But the authors were probably told not to go there. So, they didn't, as it might have led to a different outcome. For example, if the English population as a whole really cherishes, loves and values the church for the quality of *care* it provides to others (the lonely, elderly, bereaved, etc.) – through clergy, lay ministry and congregations – then we might be funnelling more resources and energy into care itself. Then sustaining it and ensuring that those who care most are also looked after and not afflicted by heaps of burdensome administration, daft targets or expectations and rubrics that actually *prevent* them from caring. In the NHS, do you want to meet a nurse who really cares and can treat you well (in all senses)? Or an efficient one, who last month met all their targets and is now being groomed in a talent pool? I guess you could have both, but if forced to choose between the two, I know whose hands I'd rather be in. If that is so for nurses, then why is it so difficult for our bishops and the authors of the *Governance Review Group Report* to write a simple sentence on the value of care? Let alone of caring for the carers.

The debate about the usefulness of the *Governance Review Group Report* lies in the questions it will not face. It won't face those questions because the current Church of England leadership are afraid of the answers. Or of discovering that the answers proposed by the leadership have no traction. Let me explain more. The oldest institution in the world is the family, or perhaps a form of marriage or partnership that produced families. This institution predates Christianity and all other major faiths. The church is, primarily, a family – albeit an extended household (*oikos* in Greek), incorporating the slave, tutor, hired hand, labourer, widow, orphan and others. Now, families have to be organized to run well. But they are not organizations. They are institutions, bound principally by fidelity, fellowship, values and love, rather than by utilitarian metrics. However, this is not an essay that pitches institution against organization and comes out in favour of organic rather than mechanistic goals.

I have already mentioned nurses, so we can say here that hospitals have to be organized, and there are aspects to their identity that are organizational. Sometimes we can only cope as a social conglomerate because there are systems where the computer says 'no', where 'you are not a priority' and where 'I lost my place on the waiting list'. Frustrating and painful though this can feel – and sometimes deeply personal, though it rarely is – we cannot negotiate social life exclusively through our individual or group-felt needs. There has to be some organizational buffer between us, in so many walks of life, and often at critical, delicate points of human existence. Organizations are like clothing: useful, often fashion-driven, basically functional and ultimately expendable.

Organizational approaches to bodies, people and groups are useful, and indeed essential. We work in them, and they work for us. However, 'the organization' will not send you a bereavement card – as the organization has no heart or hands, it can't. But someone feeling and caring within that organization might write to you and do so on its behalf. We may feel cared for by them, that this organization has been *kind*. But organizations cannot, of themselves, care. Churches are, as I say, meant to be organized, rather like families. But you know, sometimes the most unorganized families – hopeless in some respects – are the most loving and can give you the absolute best start in life. So how is it that the *Governance Review Group Report* has produced yet another offering that the flesh, soul and body of the church (clergy, parishes, congregations) will simply be recoiling from, virtually viscerally?

I suspect that this may lie in a kind of undiagnosed 'systemic disorder' prevalent in church leadership. By this term, I mean conduct characterized by difficulties in social interaction and communication, and by restricted and repetitive behaviour. It can often present as poor emotional intelligence and an apparent lack of empathy or compassion. Does the Church of England exhibit this? Yes and no. Yes, in the sense that within our Clergy Discipline Measure (CDM) processes, we have inculcated institutional disorder. Bishops – note, a primary task is care – are not allowed to care for complainants or respondents. The National Safeguarding Team (NST) has developed a veritable panoply of systemically disordered systems that somehow cut out justice, fairness, transparency and kindness, and has replaced core values with a thick crust of impenetrable bureaucracy and opacity. No one feels cared for by a Core Group. No one finds an NST process to be kind. No one thinks to ask, 'Why is the church like this here?' And yet they will have a sense that parishes, congregations, clergy and ministers are exemplary at care. Because the closer you get to where God is at work in ordinary people, the more likely it is you will encounter love, care, kindness and compassion. At this level, the church is family-like and can even be organized.

There are no real cures for systemic disorder – just the challenging work of therapies and disciplines that manage the condition. The trouble with organizations that are systemically disordered is that they are usually the last to realize it. Moreover, they often recruit leaders who copy the inherent traits of systemic disorder, and if left unchecked the organization soon becomes known for its inhumane systems and its lack of tactile care, kindness, courage and compassion. I have never been much of a fan of Avery Dulles' *Models of the Church* (1976), preferring instead the more nuanced approach of Edward LeRoy Long Jr and his *Patterns of Polity* (2001). His discussions of monarchical episcopacy, managerial episcopacy, pastoral and exemplary episcopacy would be useful for the authors of the *Governance Review Group Report*. As would Long's discussion of representative leadership, congregations, associations and what he terms 'over-structures'. Few major denominations lack these aspects. The question is, how are they blended, and in what ways is the ecclesial, political or social body conscious of them?

Let us take an example from social and political life. Social work is an active and reactive 'caring profession'. Yet it is funded by the taxpayer and regulated. Even if the authority of oversight is dispersed, there is some level at which ownership of the quality and delivery of care, and its remit and scope, is a constant. It is handled by the civil service or government department, whether local, regional or national, and the elected MP and cabinet minister who might exercise managerial, monarchical or representative oversight. As a sector, social work and social workers will respond differently to the styles of leadership that a government minister brings. But governments come and go, and there is a sense in which the constancy of this caring profession must be sustained, independent of the next minister promising to 'shake things up' in the sector, whipping it into line with last year's manifesto promises.

Popes can come and go too. But the Curia (an ecclesiastical civil service) remains. There are some good aspects to this. And there are some downsides too. A Curia that does not like a new papal agenda can drag its feet and implement change very slowly, at an almost glacial pace. New policies and priorities are easy for any pope to promote, but they are much, much harder to implement. Then there is the Church of England, which comprises over 40 dioceses, with centres of power vested in each bishop, each diocesan HQ, Church House Westminster, the Church Commissioners, General Synod, the Archbishops' Council and Lambeth Palace. Each diocese is its own charity and limited company. Centralization is difficult, and in so far as the Church of England has any kind of continuity in institutional memory, through the constancy of an equivalent to a civil service, that is now largely extinct. It may once have existed in Church House Westminster or Lambeth Palace. But successive 'episcopal governments' have reduced their powers (that is, slashing costs!), rebranded, reimagined and then reformed (again!). The result is a kind of organizational chaos that makes for the worst of all worlds, but always with the best of intentions.

If looking for an example of this, safeguarding in the Church of England is particularly apposite. The NST has little power over diocesan safeguarding functions. The performance of dioceses in this field is variable. There are some good examples of practice, but there are some atrocious ones too. The handling of recent cases of clergy suicide, and suicidal clergy who have breakdowns, is instructive here. At its centre, the Church of England would have you believe all their safeguarding is good. But it is a curate's egg: good in parts; truly terrible in others. When systemic disorder rules, the energy and resources don't go there, and are disproportionately allotted to 'making a good impression' instead. The results of this in the wider church are now easy to observe. Huge chasms emerge between rhetoric and reality, and between leaders and the led. The bridges of trust and care that once spanned those gaps were broken long ago. The bishops themselves in part caused this: they either can't, won't or don't care. They are process driven, by targets, management and strategy, imagining they are CEOs of an underperforming charity, recruitment or care agency. They tend to lead like this too, and don't seem to be *care driven*.

While I am wholly sympathetic to the problem that the *Governance Review Group Report* tried to address, the starting place for the work was fundamentally wrong. Indeed, the authors avoided the obvious fundamental ground for any further development: how is the church of today to be an expression of the body of Christ in its local community, parishes, chaplaincies, regions and nation? Instead, the authors focused on dioceses and bishops, who, let's be honest, have little impact on most churchgoers, and even in Church of England parishes are not exactly what folk spend their time thinking and talking about. I mean, when was the last time you went to church and found yourself in a lively lay-led discussion about the latest diocesan strategy, vision, motto or shiny new episcopal initiative? They might politely chat about these things when the bishop or Archdeacon comes a-calling with a sermon or visits for a charge.

Otherwise, it is business as usual on the ground, and back to caring for others with the clergy and chaplains. And yet, the new orders, glossy reports, flow diagrams that have been pulled off flip charts keep arriving in the post and inbox. What is all of this for, I wonder? Who is being served by this growing mountain of paraphernalia? Does any of it *connect* to anything? Meanwhile, the elephants in the room grow ever larger, squeezing more folk out, because someone decided sexuality, gender, poverty, climate change, racism, refugees, disability, poverty ... and fixing the hole in the church roof are less of a priority than the new Diocesan Mission Plan, which won't mention any of the above.

I have often opined that the organizational texture of the Church of England bears some relationship to the University of Oxford. What do the two have in common? Here are some observations. First, an exceedingly small central administration that is probably inadequate for a university or denomination. Second, a federal-type structure that has over three dozen colleges or dioceses, but all of varying size, age, wealth and reputation. Third, huge disparities between them in terms of power and wealth, yet some kind of centralized 'levelling up' financial system in which the richer bodies (usually resentfully) are meant to help the poorer ones. Fourth, Oxford is governed by Congregation and by Council, as the Church of England is by General Synod. Sort of. There are college fellowships (which are self-governing) just like diocesan synods, which also self-govern. Sort of. Fifth and finally, there is another centre – quite different from the first one – where the vice-chancellor or archbishops work, yet can do little on a day-to-day basis to impact how any college or diocese is actually run. When the vice-chancellor speaks for the University of Oxford, does he or she speak for St Swithun's College, founded in AD 1475? Maybe. It kind of depends on what the vice-chancellor was talking about at the time. Do the principal and fellows of St Swithun's need to take any notice of this vice-chancellor's speech? Not really. But it is a free world, and you can agree or disagree, or not bother to note it. As with the vice-chancellor, so with dioceses, bishops and archbishops.

Increasingly, the survival of the Church of England is going to come down to being truthful about its size and sustainability. Can you have dispersed authority and finances (currently the case), yet tighter central control, and an emasculated General Synod? The Methodist Church in Britain centralized as much as they could: care homes, HR, safeguarding and much else.

That has largely ensured an even quality of training, oversight and investment is delivered nationally, and it is a model the Church of England ought to consider in the future.

However, at present, for all the alleged vision of the latest Church of England governance review (that is, the *Baines Report*), it suffers from the same hubris of self-sufficiency that has dogged the Church of England for well over two centuries. I see little sign of anyone able to grasp the nettle – or indeed to know what the nettle looks like and where it is. The future for the Church of England faces some quite brutal economic choices – and some decisions will need to be made very, very soon. Indeed, those days are already upon us. But do the people running the Church of England – ecclesiocrats – understand the ecclesionomics of what we are facing? I fear they do not. Moreover, the question is not just '*Who* is running the ecclesial economy?', but also more importantly, 'For whom and for what purposes are they running it?'

The evidence of chaos, lack of accountability, monarchical episcopacy cannot be masked by endless innovation. Increasingly, we seem to encourage spin-off franchises – multiple fresh expressions, breathtaking announcements of thousands of new congregations and the like – when in truth we struggle to sustain our core business. These shiny new initiatives all have the 'C of E Brand' and sit proudly amid the aisles and in the front shop windows of diocesan HQs. But the shiny new things don't sell well, and nor do they pay their way. Is there any fresh expression – any – paying a normal parish share/quota to a diocese? The staple core 'product' subsidizes each new product launch. Yet the business is still loss-making.

The Church of England should stop doing new things and get back to what we're good at and what people valued church for. But we don't and won't. Our leaders drive us on to fresh innovations, restructuring, reform and endless reimagining. We have done this with parishes, theological education and much else. Yet the underlying problem is never addressed. We are now declining at such a rate that we need to make some hard choices. If we don't do something soon, we will become the ecclesiastical equivalent of a Debenhams or Woolworths; big places, visible in most communities, overstocked, yet immensely popular at Christmas, but not enough customers for the rest of the year, and so, ultimately, insolvent.

I mentioned nurses and hospitals earlier. One of their main roles is to look after patients. Now, there is a word with some meaning: the patient. The church is full of patients too: folk waiting for healing, blessing, care, renewal and worship. We wait patiently and expectantly, and we do so in hope. But in the meantime, the systemic disorder of the Church of England keeps us in limbo. The leadership's willed unconscious refuses to act with prescience and courage, only craving more innovation, productivity and reform.

Finally, then, some Breaking News. The Church of England does not have to exist. God can build the kingdom without us. So we need to discover why we exist. We cannot take our future in the spiritual marketplace for granted any longer. Religious consumers can manage without us – the statistics on weddings, funerals and baptisms now tell us exactly that. This is one of the reasons why the *Governance Review Group Report* is such a disappointment and a lost opportunity. Yet its fundamental flaw remains. If you are trying to reform the church and you don't start with God, it never ends well.

Reflections for Part 2

Blessed are the poor in spirit, for the kingdom of Heaven is theirs ...
Blessed are the pure in heart, for they shall see God.
(Matthew 5.3, 8)

We think of our scriptures coming to us in Greek and Hebrew, and perhaps in Latin or translated into English, but we forget that Jesus spoke in Aramaic, a Semitic language in which the sounds of words carried their meaning. One thinks, for example, of the Arabic word for 'flute': a similar sounding word to 'float', and of course the noise of a musical instrument like a flute effectively floats. When we turn to the Beatitudes, we are normally confronted with each phrase beginning 'Blessed are'.

The purpose of Jesus' Beatitudes was to complement the Ten Commandments. In some respects, we need to remember that the Ten Commandments are largely a list of 'don'ts'. In effect, the Commandments all begin with the invocation: 'Do not do this', 'Do not do that'. The Beatitudes, on the other hand, are the flip side of the coin. It's a statement about what blessing is: blessing, we should remember, is simply the activity of raising things to their proper status before God. Jesus is not abolishing the law, but he is saying that what you do with the law requires judgement and discernment. Applying the law, as Solomon knew, is a matter of wisdom.

Blessing one another with gifts or an invocation is the stuff of ordinary everyday humanity. Blessing bread and wine is setting them aside and raising them to their proper status before God. They are gifts from God and, like so many things, indeed all things, they proceed from God as gifts, and therefore the universe itself is a blessing. The rabbis used to say that God rules the universe by blessing everything – and blessing constantly, all the time. What is blessed is raised to its proper status.

My use of the tense 'raised' here is intentional, because when one looks at the Aramaic language that Jesus would have used for the Beatitudes, the word 'blessed' is not really the right word at all. There are two much better translations of the original Aramaic word with which Jesus begins each Beatitude. The first word of each Beatitude is *Tubwayhun*, and it is better understood as 'ripened' or 'mature' – describing what a believer, a mature disciple of Jesus, is to be like.

Ripened for service in the kingdom of God carries with it the implicit notion that growth is not for hurrying. Discipleship takes time to cultivate, and the Holy Spirit will develop us to ripeness and maturity over a sustained period of time. We can do what we like to tend and water, but God gives the growth. The seasons are in God's hands. But it is still by our fruits that we will be known and also judged. To be a gift to the world, we need ripening.

Maturity is a particular human quality, as well as one in nature. Mature crops, fruits and grains would be easily understood by Jesus' hearers. In the markets, there would be mature and ripe produce. Maturity is reaching the right sage of development – for ourselves, but also others. Maturity is coming of age; becoming responsible for our actions; being able to offer active service to others, whether in leadership or in active participation.

Likewise, the word 'ripe'. Ripeness was something that Jesus' hearers would have understood and been at home with immediately: ripe corn, ripe figs, unripe figs. Ripeness was something that could only be tested in its time, and it requires communal agreement as to what is ripe. Ripeness is always corporate and corporeal. Therefore, it's not the case that unripe is bad: it's just that it hasn't had the time to mature and become ripe. The strength of this is that gentle tending produces the best growth and the richest harvests. True, there is much, much hard work.

But as the soil is not abused, neither are the crops. All must be cherished into their growth.

Blessing ripens and matures. Emma Percy's poem 'Breathe' captures something of the sense of waiting, patiently, attentively, hopefully, for the ripeness to come as we draw each breath.

Breathe
Breathing is always good.
Slow, steady
Pause
Take time in responding
Calm, measured
Speak
Carefully choose the words
Truth, honesty.

Anger needs to be tempered
for righteousness' sake.
Indignation tested
for self-understanding.
Courage found to stand your ground,
for words matter.

Some things need to be said
Some voices need to be heard
Some certainties need to be challenged.

So breathe, pause, and speak.

For ripening there must be
   The plant and the soil
   The sun and the rain
   The insects to pollinate
   The careful cultivation of
   pruning and nurturing.

> Seasons must come and go
>> From buds to flowers
>> From fruit to seeds
>> The dead wood of winter
>> The new shoots of spring.

John the Baptist was mature and ripe, but he knew too that he was expendable. His life and work was to prepare the way for another who was to come. Our role in life is to be more like John the Baptist. He prays one of the few short prayers that followers of Christ will ever need: 'He must increase, but I must decrease.' John decreased and Christ increased.

John fulfilled what Jesus would later proclaim in John 12.24: 'Amen, Amen I say to you, unless a wheat grain falls into the earth *and* dies, it remains only a single grain, but if it dies it bears much fruit.' Or, as Paul would have it, they are the treasures of the church, in our earthenware pots. We carry the death of Jesus in our bodies, so God's life – matured and ripened – may be manifest in us. We are given over to death for Jesus' sake, so that the life of Jesus may be manifested in our mortal flesh. We must yield ourselves, our power, ourselves, so that what God longs to give birth to will be seeded, grow, flourish and mature. Let God ripen what the Holy Spirit has planted within you. The seed will bear fruit and be a blessing to others.

Discussion

- If we are to follow the example of John the Baptist, what must we lose in order to prepare the way and for others to gain?
- What is to decrease so that God may increase?
- What is to be cleared away so the new life can begin to bud in our communities?

PART 3

The See of Faith

6

A Critical Commentary on *A Consultation Document: Bishops and Their Ministry Fit for a New Context*

One can hardly do better than the satirical takes on the latest attempt at rebranding and reorganizing the Church of England: its governance, purpose and priorities; dioceses and where they fit in; and bishops as leaders. The latest consultation document is peppered with the familiar terms and tropes of contemporary ecclesial 'committee-speak' (e.g., support, resource, accountability, mutual, action, regional, mission), and in nearly all respects reflects the triumph of mechanistic visions for the church, replete with functional-instrumental language that is geared for reification, namely tangible signs of success and growth. If you are looking for symbolic, organic or reciprocal, contextualized models of the church, this denomination is not for you.

It is hard for most folk to put this into words. But across the land, supporters (as distinct from recognized members) are finding that church has become alien, with the day-to-day church-speak no longer connecting or making much sense. And as for inspiring us in wonder, to contemplate or critically reflect, well, that boat sailed some time ago and it is now ploughing its own furrows in different seas.

If you read this document, you get the picture quite quickly. Theology is (as usual), a casualty: MIA or AWOL (missing in action or absent without leave). The functionality with which such consultation documents are concerned betrays the anxieties of the authors. God is something to be marketed and sold. More sales lead to more success and growth, which affirms the original endeavour.

This hermeneutic is hard to question and even harder to break. This leads the church down its own rabbit hole. Culture must be engaged with, but only as a means to an end, which is a project devoted to success and growth of the church. In commercial terminology, this is not even akin to a customer survey or a marketing questionnaire. Church leaders don't seriously want to hear from the public about how it might improve services to the community or learn critical lessons *from* culture that challenge and change the service provider. No. The drivers of such functionality simply strive for better techniques that deliver what they believe the public require. Such leaders forget that commitment is voluntary and fluid, faith optional and belief varied.

The essence of the *Bishops and Their Ministry Fit for a New Context* is a mooted shift from spatial episcopal oversight to one that is situational and subject based. A number of commentators have had some mirth with 'Bishop for Brexit' (surely, according to Boris Johnson, this is already done?), climate change, education and the like. Something of this already exists. There is a 'Lead Bishop' in debates within the House of Lords on higher education (until recently, the Bishop of Winchester).

Yet to the best of my knowledge, there is no episcopal House of Lords equivalent for further education. Should this matter? Yes. The percentage of people in further education from Asian, Black, mixed-heritage and other ethnic groups increased from 19.3 per cent to 22.6 per cent in the last five years. There are well over one million more students in further education than higher education in England, and the opportunities that arise from further education and higher education have an important story to tell about social division and economic opportunity in the UK. That said, let us not forget that the Church of England and its bishops in the House of Lords only have relevance to

English affairs. The structures and practices of higher education in Wales is similar to England, but not to Scotland or Northern Ireland.

As we have mentioned Brexit, it would be unwise to ignore the potential for overlapping episcopal oversight that is likely to emerge, including areas that may stoke confusion or even conflict. My reading of the *Bishops and Their Ministry Fit for a New Context* is that it envisages a kind of fusion model of government by cabinet with the familiar ethos of episcopal kyrierarchy. If power and authority shift from the ground (spatial) to the situational and subject based, the net result will be inherently non-local and anti-democratic. The business of representation – whether accountable or symbolic – will shift to arenas where bishops have designated responsibility and opinions. Or perhaps bishops may go further and claim vicarious expertise on behalf of the church and its collective members.

I think this is misguided and muddled and will lead to confusion and conflicts within the church. For example, does the Bishop for Agriculture and Fisheries connect up with the Bishops for Rural Affairs, or Foreign Affairs, and/or Brexit? Is the row about the English fishing industry – I am not denying its crucial importance – located in the rights and concerns of those working in the industry; or territorial waters and quotas; or sustainability, climate change and ecological concerns? Which bishop has the right knowledge and experience for this brief? Moreover, the next time a spat breaks out between English fishermen (note, not Welsh, Scottish or Irish) and their French or Spanish counterparts, is this a Brexit issue, or indeed Foreign (or Home?) Affairs, to say nothing of Agriculture and Fisheries?

Readers of the *Consultation Document* may also worry about how subject areas and situations become priorities or deemed to be more subordinate. The armed services have a bishop already. Should the police and the emergency services be placed on the same representational footing? Policing in England is by region, with Scottish policing distinct and separate. Similar devolved powers and identities have crystallized in health care. Coastguards are more complex. Most of the media is regulated by Ofcom, but that covers the UK, not just England. Does the *Consultation Document* envisage bishops commenting – morally or in any censorial capacity – on press, television, cinema or other public output? It should be noted this has not usually stopped Church of England bishops before – they have often lapsed into 'speaking for the nation' – forgetting that their remit is England, not the entire UK.

We might also note the inherent hierarchies ascribed within government by cabinet. Let us take the Department for Health and Social Care as an example. Currently, it includes more junior ministers for care and mental health, vaccines and public health, patient safety and primary care, and others with supporting roles in aspects of social health. Likewise, the Department for Work and Pensions covers disabled people, well-being, disability policy and equality, welfare delivery ... and of course employees of the NHS, including nurses, doctors and paramedics. Given the overlapping responsibility and potential for conflicts of interest inherent in government for individuals and groups alike, any of whom may belong to several of the categories just noted, any attempt by the churches to funnel constituents and their concerns into one single silo is at best naive and, at worst, asinine.

I suspect that the Church of England – unable to manage sexuality, gender, equality, safeguarding and other basic social givens – is *not* 'oven-ready' (as Boris Johnson might also have falsely promised) to relaunch itself on an unsuspecting nation with some panoramic remit to offer commentary and guidance on issues and subjects it lacks the expertise to speak on, or the authority to even opine about. In any case, this would require heavy resourcing from high-calibre advisers, which, currently, the Church of England lacks. But such is the inherent hubris of the *Consultation Document* that it cannot reflect on how alien and intrusive this new model of episcopal organization would be perceived to be by the wider public. Moreover, there is an element of motes and beams (Matthew 7.1–5) in many of the issues that the Church of England has historically ascended its own national pulpit to declaim upon. Any rights to such sermonizing have to be earned and are not to be presumed.

We saw some evidence for this in the recent ticking off the Church of England's Ethical Investment Advisory Group (EIAG) gave to investment companies in their May 2021 publications to the National Investing Bodies (NIBs). The EIAG chided other bodies – international human rights should be respected by the companies in which they invest. Clearly nobody briefed the EIAG that on gender, sexuality, equality and employment rights, the Church of England had in fact opted out of the 1998 Human Rights Act decades earlier, precisely so it could continue to affirm and support the very discrimination that the 1998 HRA sought to outlaw.

Hence, a clergyperson in the Church of England who engages in same-sex marriage with their beloved partner is not at liberty to use the 1998 legislation. The Church of England's and House of Bishops' position remains as 'these are good and proper laws for the people of this nation to follow, but they are not for those of us who belong to and preside over the church'. In a similar vein, Justin Welby delivered a meek rebuttal of the Anglican Church in Ghana, which threw its weight behind the Promotion of Proper Human Sexual Rights and Ghanaian Family Values Bill (2021), which would criminalize same-sex relations and even make it a crime to simply advocate for LGBT+ rights, punishable by up to a decade in jail. The Archbishop of Canterbury felt he could not do more than chide the Anglican Church of Ghana, as he argued his authority was confined to English affairs. He had presumably forgotten his censure and banning of the Episcopal Church of the USA, which accepted same-sex marriages, and in a country where they are lawful. It is unclear why the Archbishop can intervene decisively and quite punitively in the USA but not extend a parallel censure to Ghana.

I strongly suspect that the deep anxieties and paralysing fears of bishops, and their palpable sense of utter disarray, is rooted in this latest attempt to reorganize and rebrand. Bishops have lost sight of their primary purpose, calling and function. That is, being kind and good shepherds, wise teachers, encouraging the faithful, supporting the weak, alleviating the suffering and pains of the poor and broken, and being to their clergy, congregation, churches and all people as Christ is to others.

In the final comments below, I wish to acknowledge my gratitude to Gerald Hiestand and Todd Wilson (*The Pastor as Theologian*, 2015), and Kevin Vanhoozer and Owen Strachan (*The Pastor as Public Theologian*, 2015). With them, I express a humble hope for the Church of England: that it will begin to recover poise and courage, and somehow find the heart and mind to recover that simple vocation – embody love, mercy, kindness, wisdom and care for all (for God so loved the world).

Bishops are to mediate the wisdom and compassion of God: to be teachers and pastors, after the example of Christ himself, no less. Bishops, together with the churches and communities they serve, are too often held captive by models of leadership. The bishop as a pre-eminent pastor-theologian is a particular kind of generalist: one who specializes in viewing all of life from the perspective of what God was, is and will do in Jesus Christ. Nowadays, many bishops (and clergy) see themselves as missional target-setters, motivational practitioners and middle managers, presiding over a dysfunctional organization that needs (their) reform.

The history and tradition of the church does not recognize this vision for episcopacy and should refuse it. To save the soul of the church, bishops need to return to a *love* of theology, not just a nodding acquaintance with a few bright ideas. The office of bishop (and theologian) are not recent innovations or an executive position. These roles have ancestry in the leadership offices of ancient Israel: prophets, priests, judges and rulers. Jesus commissioned the office of pastor: it continues Jesus' ministry as the good shepherd of the new covenant community and as someone who embodies wisdom, inspired by the Spirit. Bishops are a particular embodiment of this ministry.

Without theological vision, the people perish. Managers can help implement such vision. But it is not the task of managers to set out the vision for the people and proclaim their strategy and tactics as some kind of gospel or missional blueprint. That is not the good news. Being a bishop is not an ecclesiastical 'job'. It is, rather, an 'occupation'. Bishops are to be occupied with God (for which they need theology and spirituality), and then to be occupied with what preoccupies God's heart and mind – the cares and concerns Christ has for our broken world and its needy people (engaging in pastoral care). Thus occupied, a bishop might then occupy some place (usually referred to as a diocese) and live out their vocation in much the same way that Jesus dwelt among us. For God so loved the *world* that he sent his only Son (John 3.16), fully occupied with God, to be an occupant in a small, neglected corner of an empire. Jesus was preoccupied with the poor, lonely, diseased, disabled and oppressed. Thus abiding, Jesus made his abode (home) among us, serving, leading, healing, preaching, and giving and receiving hospitality. Likewise, he invites bishops to dwell in particular times and places, radiating the same love, compassion and wisdom of God.

7

The Modern Myth of Impartiality: What the BBC and the Church of England Have in Common

We can all buy into the importance and value of impartial, fair, neutral, unbiased and balanced assessments. We expect our systems of justice to provide nothing less. No one wants to be on trial in a court riddled with prejudice, bias and conflicts of interest. We expect our broadcasters to inform us. We do not watch the news to be groomed into thinking or acting in a particular way. (Should you covet a political slant on a subject, buy a newspaper.) In the church, we expect pastoral care to be available to one and all. So we offer chaplaincy to the prisoner, giving our equal care to any victim of their crime.

Institutions and individuals carry the duties and cargoes of social and moral responsibility. However, even before one begins to comprehend the values and behaviours we carry on behalf of society for human flourishing, we have to start with a simple basic self-critical epiphany. It is this: it is not possible, ever, to be non-judgemental. That is why law courts exist, journalists record and report what they believe to be important (thereby excluding the peripheral), and churches are not communities that have any business in or vocation to always be balanced.

Counsellors recognize that, whenever they are engaged in therapy, each nod, facial expression, attention to this word, incident or experience, or dwelling on this or that encounter, is, per se, a judgement call. Any claim to be non-judgemental lacks existential realization. We simply cannot function, as humans, without our inner maps and filters. They conduct our affairs of the heart, our rational processing and our day-to-day decisions. These are complex, social, shared, personal, quirky, wise, irrational, feeling and unfeeling. Humans judge. They are partial. We may strive for balance and harmony, but that in itself is a decision, bound to be based on our perceptions and, yes, some bias. How could it not be so?

The BBC states that its mission is 'to act in the public interest, serving all audiences through the provision of impartial, high-quality and distinctive output and services which inform, educate and entertain'. Journalism, much like the working definition of implicit religion coined by Edward Bailey, is a matter of 'intensive concerns resulting in extensive effects'. But all foci of such concerns are filtered through prior lenses of discernment, deliberation and judgement. For this reason, I hold that institutions acting in the public interest are obliged to be open-minded but not neutral or impartial. In fact, the very nature of public interest requires education and information, contributing to formation of individuals and communities in citizenship and the fostering of collective social and moral responsibility.

We usually regard impartiality as not favouring one position or person over another, and being free of bias. Likewise, we usually associate partiality with favouritism, bias or even one-sidedness. To be fair-minded in a given contest is to be even-handed, and we will expect this of any referee or adjudication. To be biased is to be more inclined to one side than another. Balance is usually taken to mean being fair, equal and proportionate, such that one proposition or person does not outweigh or dominate the others. The very scales of justice are meant to reflect this.

Neutrality is overrated. To be neutral is to take neither side in a dispute, nor to be involved in a conflict that needs to be resolved, or even in setting some direction. 'Neutral' can also mean (literally) to be disengaged (for example, an idle vehicle, motionless).

In terms of civic, social and moral responsibility, it is neither possible nor desirable for our public institutions – whether a museum, the NHS, BBC or the Church of England – to be neutral or impartial. After all, consider that when a visitor enters Broadcasting House, their eyes are often drawn to the BBC's motto, inscribed beneath its coat of arms above the entrance. It reads, 'Nation shall speak peace unto nation.' This motto extends back to the BBC's original formation on 1 January 1927, when it was adopted by the new Corporation to signify the purpose of the new broadcaster (post-empire?). It is often said that the motto was derived from an adaptation from the book of Micah (4.3): 'Nation will not lift up sword against nation, no longer will they learn to make war.'

Public institutions exist to perpetuate particular moral, civic and social public values down the ages, quite independent of their actual popularity at any given time. The Church of England, as with any national church, also deals in public religious values. We expect these institutions to be propositional, but also open-minded. They must also aspire to be proactive and reactive, steady and stable, yet also evolve. They have a commitment to being diagnostic, prognostic and analytical in what they represent, as well as carrying what we might term 'soft values' (that is, behavioural, dispositional, etc.), which in turn will govern the inner-implicit conduct of that institution.

Kindness, care, attentiveness and accessibility will nest in with the curiosity, critical appraisal, patience, doggedness, endeavour and resilience that is needed. And finally, let me also put some markers down for courage, fortitude, resistance, protest and dissent. Can we also expect institutions like the BBC or the Church of England not just to reflect or report on social and political values, but also to question them and sometimes even publicly rebuke them?

One remarkable modern example of such agency in the twenty-first century took place in Ukraine in 2004, when the opposition politician Victor Yushchenko was campaigning for the presidency. He suddenly became gravely ill and, as we now know, he had been poisoned (as a result of which, and to this day, he remains facially disfigured). Despite this, he was resolved to continue as a candidate.

On election day, a few weeks after his poisoning, Yushchenko was leading by a significant margin in the votes. Suspicions were therefore raised when the ruling party announced themselves as the victors, briefing the state-owned TV station to run the line: 'Ladies and gentlemen, we announce that the challenger, Victor Yushchenko, has been decisively defeated.'

However, during this live transmission, a translator for the deaf community, Natalia Dmytruk, at the side of the TV screen broadcast, was suddenly faced with a stark moral choice. Should she translate what was being read and said, or communicate what everyone really knew? She chose hope, and with considerable courage Dmytruk refused to translate the scripted words of state TV. Instead, she signed: 'I'm addressing all the deaf citizens of Ukraine ... they are lying and I'm ashamed to translate those lies ... Yushchenko is our President.'

Many, many deaf viewers and sign-language users were startled by the disruptive contrast in scripted words being said and read by the newsreader, and Dmytruk signing in the corner of the screen. Viewers moved to action by this courageous act of resistance began to contact their friends, families and networks to raise awareness of Dmytruk's message. This in turn moved journalists and the media to investigate and interrogate the events surrounding the election. The Orange Revolution began soon after, when a million people dressed in orange descended on the capital, Kiev, to protest against the fraudulent outcome of the election. Held to account by the people, the ruling party were forced to hold a new election, in which Yushchenko was declared the rightful winner.

Promoting balance, neutrality or impartiality in order to keep the peace is neither right nor fair to any of the interested parties. Imagine for a moment King Solomon (see 1 Kings 3.16–28) saying to two mothers upon the death of one infant and the ensuing custody battle raging over the remaining child, 'Look, I can see you are both grief-stricken and hurt, and you might both have legitimate claims. So, how about coming to some kind of co-parenting or child-sharing arrangement, where the infant lives with one mother for half the week and then goes to the other mother for the remaining half? That way, nobody loses. The child can then decide who it wants to be with when it has come of age.' There is a certain 'balance' and neutrality here. We may praise Solomon for his impartiality. Yet in our reimagined scenario, asked to referee this dispute, he prevaricates; then declares a score draw, and does not make the *decision* required.

For King Solomon in the Temple, try and read Bishop Solomon in the Church of England. Faced with a highly charged emotional dispute – doubtless with tears, shouting and screaming with two mothers fighting over one baby – the bishop instinctively opts for defusing the situation with pastoral pragmatism and empathy. The bishop lays aside the obligations of truth and justice and instead compliments him- or herself on their pastoral pragmatism.

You can almost envisage this catastrophe in slow motion. What is a bishop to do with this screaming match and utterly awful situation? In the absence of a DNA test, the episcopal answer is *neutrality* – assuring both women of 'prayers and empathy at this difficult time' – and then a neat compromise that is nice to both bereft mothers. Some pastoral genius is surely at work here? Er, no: sadly not.

We should recoil at this quirky rendering of the story, although it has a familiarity – exactly the kind of compromise and fudge that a group of English Anglican bishops would manufacture. But it does not exhibit wisdom. Impartiality is not what the Old Testament extols. Wisdom is 'other', and it requires thought, calm and decisive care, and sound judgement. Wisdom requires comprehending moral agency, acting with courage, compassion and resolve. Wisdom must sometimes be brave. Some decisions and judgements that must be made cannot please all those we care for.

Parenting works on similar premises every day (almost). Most partnerships and marriages have some experience of this too. In fact, all good relationships have to be able to handle truth in proportion to the love, value and power that is vested in a bond. When truth cannot be spoken for fear of upset or disturbing the peace (which usually means the status quo), we are seldom well served by neutrality or impartiality.

Yet putting impartiality into day-to-day practice is more difficult than it might at first appear. Like Ofcom, the BBC's Editorial Guidelines require 'due impartiality', which gives some licence to a more nuanced and interpretive approach:

> The term 'due' means that the impartiality must be adequate and appropriate to the output, taking account of the subject and nature of the content, the likely audience expectation and any signposting that may influence that expectation.[1]

The Guidelines go on to say that 'news in whatever form must be treated with due impartiality ...' (*Editorial Guidelines*, 2019, 4.3.10). Thus, impartiality properly understood can enable those confronted with difficult judgements, which can be particularly complex when dealing with causes concerning contested moral issues.

There is a further complication to factor in at this juncture, namely social media. Most developed nations can bear painful testimony to moral debates that have been driven more by tone than content, and more by emotive reactions than by reason. The debate on abortion in Ireland, gun control in the USA, Brexit in the UK, and sexuality in the Church of England all come to mind.

With the cultural elevation of 'my truth' or 'alternative facts', the quality of debate inevitably suffers, and also the very reasons for it. Mainstream media can be culpable in this too. In 2016, many local and regional USA TV stations found that covering a Donald Trump campaign event on their patch during the election turned out to be 'TV gold' – higher audience figures and therefore increased advertising revenues. Even if the TV coverage was scornful, the ominous fascination and focus of the media gaze gave Trump the unrivalled visibility he craved. The TV networks knew this, but found the allure of a 'Trumpaign Bling Spectacle' too much to resist.

The line between news and entertainment is thinner than it once was. I can offer a brief personal anecdote here. Invited to be part of a debate on Radio Four some years ago in relation to the Church of England's 'ambivalent' stance on same-sex relationships and equal marriage, I agreed. However, I asked the researcher organizing the programme where they proposed to get an academic representing the alternative viewpoints. In asking the question, I suggested that this could not be a debate in the conventional sense, as the perspectives would be using entirely different frames of reference. I tried to explain the problems inherent in creating an 'impartial balance' in religious affairs that might be problematic in politics (for example, always ensuring a BNP spokesperson was represented on BBC's *Question Time*).

Put another way, the BBC, as broadcaster, has a responsibility for 'due impartiality', but that 'due' cannot mean treating all opinions as even, let alone equally valuable. That said, the BBC Radio Four researcher replied to me, somewhat to my alarm, that although she knew the proposed slot in the programme did not (strictly speaking) 'work' as a debate, listeners would nonetheless be enthralled and entertained by the inevitable argument. So I explained I needed to decline the invitation, as it could never be a debate between two positions of moral equity, and that to set the debate up in this framework could only diminish one perspective, while unreasonably dignifying the other with an esteem that was questionable.

News requires a degree of objectivity, subjectivity, analysis, education and edge. Where possible, the facts should be allowed to speak for themselves. Yet they still require contextualization, presentation and explanation, which is partly why the value of 'due impartiality' is not to be underestimated. We should also pay due homage to the courageousness of many journalists who risk life and limb in covering news and current affairs. They can often find themselves in serious danger for seeking the truth and exposing the corruption, violence, exploitation, malfeasance and lies that keep a few in power at the expense of many, or maintain the status quo because the cost of questioning it is deemed to be too high, and individuals and institutions are unwilling to meet the expense.

History teaches us that if we capitulate to this kind of venal culture, we will be at the mercy of Pavlov's proverbial dogs. As Hannah Arendt has taught us, the banality of evil is ever-present, and an unhealthy cultural climate of populism fostered by our leaders is more like to lead to exploitation than liberation. A state of 'truth decay' is all around us, and within us too. Populism can quickly decompose into polarization, atomization and eventual segregation. A defence or recovery of impartiality is important, but it is not enough. Christian social ethics, at even the most basic level, teaches that truth can set us free. We need our social institutions to be fundamentally rooted in the truths and values that they contribute to society. Institutions that put their reputations before truth, accountability, justice and transparency risk eroding the trust that should be vested in them. And more worryingly, trust itself, part of our shared stock of social capital, decays and depletes.

Journalists and media organizations possess moral and social agency, and therefore have a stake in maintaining a flourishing society or in helping to drive social change. We referenced Natalia Dmytruk earlier, because sometimes moral courage is required to pierce the mythos of impartiality in order to speak truth to power. The true value of impartiality lies in its commitment to objectivity and facts, even though no person can escape the shadow of their subjectivity. Ethical communication recognizes imperatives of honesty, integrity, trust, truth and transparency, and will work against the forces of culture, politics and religion that seek to occlude.

Some competing convictions should never be set within a construction or facade of some faux-balanced debate. Sometimes it is simply not responsible to be neutral. Set within such a framework, impartiality is worthy if it is inferring objectivity, truthfulness, communication and education. People will need to be free to make up their own minds. That is why respectful, informed debate and analysis is the bedrock for all our great public institutions, whether that is Parliament, the BBC or the Church of England.

In Malcolm Gladwell's compelling sociological monograph, *The Tipping Point* (2000), he remarks that ultimately it is contempt that finally destroys an institution. When we cease to respect the leaders, symbols or very foundations of any institution – its purpose and values – the ensuing lack of trust is deeply corrosive for all future relationships. (This is what topples regimes, leads to revolutions and revolts, or simmering socio-political resentment and rebellion.) Institutions function to be purveyors of reliable norms, values and patterns of behaviour. When these are betrayed or disregarded, the very foundations of civilizations and societies can be shaken. Institutions cannot be taken for granted, and they need to be cherished – but not falsely cossetted – for their value in the currency of our social capital.

When the people sense their government or leaders are choosing to regard or treat their fellow citizens with contempt, the seeds of uprising are abundantly sown. When bishops and church leaders treat the laity as mere pew-fodder, or mere statistics in pie and flow charts flecked with potential, then perhaps as malleable consumers to merchandize and experiment on with new products and ideas, or just another round of disappointing results, you can begin to scent rebellion.

An institution – whether it be a government, Parliament, the police, a university, school, health or social service, church, or indeed a marriage – can survive most crises. It can usually cope with competing convictions and can even flourish with them if each party stays faithful and true to the other, their greater good and the future and integrity of that institution. But it rarely survives contempt. That is, contempt for the public and people it serves.

Good and honest disagreement – *adiaphora* – has a role in preventing bad argument and fracture on non-essential issues. Unity need not mean uniformity. There is a very real difference between dissent and contempt. Dissent has an important and honoured role within institutions. Little else can keep power accountable other than the capacity and courage for others to proclaim truth. To be blunt, dissension often 'keeps impartiality honest', and as such is to be carefully nourished and valued. Institutions deal in established norms, patterns and paradigms for behavioural relations that express good values and practices. Truth-telling and loyal dissent enables us to begin to see and learn from the difference and diversity around us.

It may well be a familiar trope, but we are all schooled into a knowledge that the only thing necessary for the triumph of evil is good people doing nothing. President John F. Kennedy thought so, and he attributed this maxim to Edmund Burke. John Stuart Mill also used the expression, and in 1916 the maxim appeared in a more polished version from the American, the Revd Charles Frederic Aked, calling for temperance restrictions on the use of alcohol. While we may quibble with the variable standards of taste, decency and probity of any given era, I venture to suggest that what we count as courage may be more of a constant.

But courage can be costly, and especially when challenging the status quo and interrogating the prevalent social construction of reality. In such circumstances we are rarely assisted by a stance berthed in neutrality or impartiality. Rather, we need a hermeneutic of suspicion, mixed with determination and resolve to surface the truth, to call power to account and to help others walk free and unafraid. Some of our most momentous breakthroughs in modern history were initiated by the bravery of a few journalists in the face of a neutered impartiality that was complicit with corruption. The courage of a few can bring about revolutionary change.

The journalist Daphne Caruana Galizia was murdered in Malta in October 2017 after a career spent exposing the links between government and organized crime. Natalia Dmytruk took an extraordinary risk in Ukraine during 2004. In the 1970s, journalists at the centre of exposing scandals such as Watergate (*Washington Post* reporters Bob Woodward and Carl Bernstein) and Spotlight (*Boston Globe* reporters Walter 'Robby' Robinson and Michael Rezendes) paid heavy prices for their determination. Maria Ressa (Philippines) and Dmitry

Muratov (Russia) both received Nobel prize awards in 2021 for their fights for freedom of expression in countries where reporters faced persistent attacks, harassment and killings.

More recently, BBC social affairs correspondent Liz MacKean and BBC producer Meirion Jones, in their dogged investigation of Jimmy Savile's history of abuse, and their pursuit of truth and justice for his victims, had to take on the BBC in order to bring out the truth of their own institution's complicity. Whether it is the courts, police, hospitals, churches or even families, the whistle-blower, victim or complainant, will often be sidelined and labelled as a deviant. They are disbelieved. Over Jimmy Savile, the BBC behaved just as other institutions initially do.

Likewise, and within the institutional church, we will struggle to remember the rank-and-file church leaders who meekly accepted oppression of the poor, the indiscriminate bombing of civilians or politically sanctioned systemic racism. But we will remember the names of Oscar Romero, George Bell and Desmond Tutu. Exemplars of courage, wisdom, virtue and truth tend to avoid neutrality and impartiality. Sometimes the price of peace is just too high.

Most of our cherished institutions know they will not merit support without demonstrating truthful capacity. They must embody integrity, probity and honesty. They cannot easily survive if they fail in this mission, as this will indicate contempt or duplicity towards their own core values, their colleagues and public. If institutions blame others for their own fiascos, or refuse to accept responsibility for their failures, this only adds to the sense of the governors, trustees or leaders serving themselves. Reputation management can be as futile and foolish as the very first garments fashioned from fig leaves. Jesus implores his disciples to engage in open and fearless speech: '… do not be afraid of them. Everything now covered up will be uncovered, and everything now hidden will be made clear' (Matthew 10.26). The BBC knows this, but I'm less sure that many Church of England bishops have clocked it. And so they continue to grasp for fig leaves.

Coda: Ecclesiastes 3
From The 2050 Amplified Version of the Bible for a Post-Viral Planet

There is:
A time for tweeting and posting
And a time for pausing and pondering
A time to react quickly
And a time for considered refrain
A time to buy for yourself
And a time to save for others
There is a time to stare into a mirror
And a time to reflect more deeply
A time to endorse
And a time to protest
A time to consent
And a time to dissent
A time for plenty
And a time for thrift
A time to accept the status quo
And a time to rise up and revolt
A time to comply
And a time to challenge
A time to breach and break
And a time to repair and restore
A time for the poor (for they are always with you)
And time for the rich to notice them (eventually)
A time to store your stuff
And a time to give away (you can't take it with you)
A time to criticize and complain
And a time to care and comfort.

There is always, always
an eternity of truth and justice,
kindness and compassion
worth striving for and sharing.
There is all of this that must be.

There is also what may endure
that is futile and foolish.
Yet we should endeavour to live in hope.
For everything, there is a reason.
To everything, there is a season.

Note

1 BBC, Editorial Guidelines, 2019, 4.1, www.bbc.co.uk/editorial guidelines/guidelines/impartiality/ (accessed 25.11.2022).

8

Crown, Constitution and Church: The Contemporary Crisis for English Religion[1]

One has to start with the numbers, and they are brutal. All Christian denominations are continuing to experience numerical decline. This now includes Evangelicals, Charismatics and Pentecostals, who have had to contend not only with fewer adherents but also the marked changes in intensity of belief and commitment.

For some decades, the outlook for religious belief in England has been a case of decidedly mixed weather. The chill winds of secularization and consumerism have impacted religious attendance and observance. A greater pluralization of non-Christian religions has led to growing demands for less privilege and more equality. Within churches, there is atomization, fragmentation and individualism, turbocharged by increasingly heated debates on sexuality, gender and ethnicity.

There is a generational crisis brewing too. Few under the age of 35 subscribe to a faith or belong to a church. Many self-define as 'spiritual, but not religious'. Values have become their new faith. They are formed out of a simple equation: Ideologies + Passions = Values. We are in the midst of a cultural climate change. Debates that once seemed settled – even with civil 'agree-to-disagree' concordats (for example on abortion) – are now subject to heated exchanges, with others frozen out of dialogue through no-platforming.

Values may well be the new religion of the twenty-first century. By values, I mean integrity, transparency, fairness, justice, truth, accountability, care, kindness and honesty. Institutions and organizations that fail to exemplify these are unlikely to be trusted by most of the under-35s. The Church of England consistently flops all tests on this. Its failure to address sexism, homophobia, systemic opacity, the lack of clear and accountable governance – well, you do the maths. Few will join. The emerging generation will get behind movements that address the political, ethical and global challenges society faces. This excludes most churches.

Churches and cultural climate change

The earliest written record of the King Canute myth comes from *Historia Anglorum* (twelfth century). Canute, to illustrate his lack of kingly power to his fawning subjects, spoke to the rising tide, commanding it to rise no further. But the sea came up as usual, drenching the King's legs.

Churches, likewise, have been unable to stem the cultural tides of modernity. Forecasts of rates of decline based on current data suggest that Welsh Presbyterianism, the Church in Wales and the United Reformed Church (the result originally of an amalgamation of English Presbyterians and Congregationalists in 1972) could become extinct by the 2030s. Scottish Episcopalians, Welsh Independents, Methodists and many Baptist congregations may be extinct by the 2040s.

Of course, such forecasts are merely extrapolations of current trends. They are not predictions and action yet to be taken could well slow or even reverse decline. Nonetheless, forecasts which suggest the extinction of both the Roman Catholic Church and the Church of England in the 2060s demonstrate the sheer scale of a problem where only the hardy Open Brethren may survive until the 2090s.

The UK's 2021 Census is yet to be reported, but given that many congregations are indicating significant declines in attendance post-Covid, it seems unlikely that these gathering clouds will have any silver linings. If Australian trends are anything to go by, and established now for some decades, then the scale of decline reported recently for the Australian 2021 Census may be a reliable precursor. Answers to a voluntary section of the Australian Census saw a 93 per cent response rate and a near doubling of 'no religion'. Fewer than half (44 per cent) identified as Christian, as opposed to the 61 per cent of 2011.

Both Roman Catholic and Church of England numbers have declined steeply to 20 and 10 per cent respectively (Roman Catholics have long been the larger group). Australian figures are in fact some way behind British experience, where the most recent surveys suggest that more than 50 per cent already are prepared to say they have no religion.

One of the great difficulties for all declining churches is that their decay is not the result of hostility but indifference. The latter works silently and unseen and, apart from organized secularism (whose importance churches wildly exaggerate), produces neither evident enemies nor approachable prospects for membership.

Crown, church and constitution

With a sharp decline in affiliation (of any kind) to the Church of England, and a rising tide of cultural disenchantment with its leaders, a constitutional crisis is now emerging. Over the past decades, the Church of England has invested significant effort in branding, marketing, mission and reorganization. Evangelistic initiatives such as 'Call to the Nation' (1975) and the 'Decade of Evangelism' (1988 onwards) proved ineffective and even counter-productive. Every initiative has seen greater public distancing from the Church of England and a steeper decline in attendance.

Rather as with a political party that cannot step outside its own bubble, the public no longer support or trust a body that does not seem credible or relevant to their daily lives, much less have anything to offer in terms of hope. The Church of England continues to discriminate on grounds of sexuality and gender. As an organization, it has a poor record on accountability, transparency, fairness and integrity. It spends time and money trying ever-harder to recruit loyal members, and yet continues, every day, to alienate more voters. Public support is crumbling. There is no appetite for a church that embodies privilege and power to discriminate while lacking proper accountability or transparency.

The most direct concern this presents in the next few years is the status of the Church of England, where the UK's constitutional monarchy's hereditary head of state must satisfy certain religious tests. Monarchs cannot be Roman Catholics (although since 2013 they can be married to one), have to be 'in communion' with the Church of England, swear an oath that they are faithful Protestants, and at coronation swear both to rule justly and to defend the rights and privileges of the Church of England.

As supreme governor of that church, the monarch makes – on the advice of ministers – all the senior appointments. Twenty-six of the 43 diocesan bishops by seniority of see sit in the House of Lords. The only other country in the world where religious leaders sit in the legislature as of right is Iran, with Shia clerics both in government and legislature.

The Gordian knot represented in these arrangements is normally referred to as 'establishment'. The Church of England is regulated by law and reflects a historically close partnership with the state where originally there was religious uniformity. That is, all citizens had to belong to the church and there was active persecution of Roman Catholics and other Christian minorities, a system which was gradually relaxed.

During the last century, the church has become increasingly autonomous to the extent that the current arrangements have been termed 'weak' establishment. The central core of establishment remains the church's continuing special relationships with the head of state, Parliament and the government of the day. To the extent that the church retains unique privileges in comparison with any other religious organizations, it can be said that the UK has religious freedom – but, embarrassingly, not religious equality.

The axis of equality and privilege is particularly troubling for the Church of England at present. The House of Lords is one half of Parliament for the UK. But there are no Welsh, Irish or Scottish denominations represented in the upper chamber. What is the argument for the Lords Spiritual in a United Kingdom where power and governance are increasingly devolved? The SNP does not nominate peers to the upper chamber. Yet we have English bishops voting on Scottish affairs and on matters that affect the union as a whole.

For example, on 15 June 2020 the House of Lords debated the Government's 'Abortion (Northern Ireland) Regulations 2020'. The Bishop of Carlisle (lead bishop on health and social affairs in Parliament) spoke in favour of an amendment negating the Regulations. In subsequent votes, he and other male bishops voted against the bill.

Who exactly was the bishop representing in these debates? Certainly not women from Northern Ireland, forced to travel across the Irish Sea if they needed a termination, and with whom he has no locus. Was his opinion in line with the Church of England's position, which says abortion though regrettable can be justified? (Actually, no.) Was he representing rank-and-file churchgoers or the population of the country (England only)? Yet he spoke and voted as of right. Imagine some parallel universe, in which a Roman Catholic bishop was always entitled to sit as one of the nine justices on the US Supreme Court, voting on abortion rights influencing legislation (for example, Roe vs Wade). Then again, maybe not.

The future of the Church of England

On current form, it is hard to imagine the Church of England making the cut for the passenger list for the proverbial Noah's Ark. Surviving any world-engulfing flood would seem improbable to most of us. For any institution even hoping to endure through floods brought about by contemporary cultural climate challenges, serious attention would need to be paid to the prevailing weather patterns and challenging winds of change. At present, all the indications point to a Church of England unable to read the signs of the times.

The vast majority of citizens in the Global North expect transparency, fairness, equality and accountability from their institutions as prerequisites for trust and investment. Most of our public institutions have understood this, adapted and changed. However, churches have been slower. Accommodating discriminatory views on gender and sexuality plays badly with the vast majority of UK citizens, and the Church of England's declining membership – present and future forecasts – suggest growing disinvestment and disenchantment.

Hanging on to power and privilege by right – but no longer by reason or reputation – is the ground on which the Church of England has pitched its tent. But that ground looks increasingly shaky and vulnerable. What is the role of one established denomination, and of only one nation, set within a devolved union? Can bishops in the House of Lords authentically represent the plethora of opinions within their own denomination on issues such as sexuality, let alone speak for the nation?

Locally, the grounded ministry of churches and clergy in parishes and chaplaincies continues to be valued and cherished. But valued locally engaged service – spiritual, pastoral, civic – does not require the trappings and trimmings of establishment. Yet somehow the current leadership of the Church of England assumes that establishment is an 'all-or-nothing' equation. Casting an eye around the rest of Europe, there are many examples of national churches that do not require the privileges of establishment.

Reading the signs of the times requires grounded realism, upon which the seeds of hope might germinate. Alas, it is the antithesis of this that currently reigns in the Church of England, with the senior leadership entirely besotted with gibberish, masquerading as visionary.

Recently, a friend and colleague of mine – a senior cleric in a diocese that has a lengthy coastline – was surprised to be invited to a presentation by the newly formed Mission

Enabling Team. Maps, charts, vision statements and mission action plans were unfurled with great fanfare. Apparently, by 2035, the old rural deaneries were to be replaced with missional hubs. Parishes would be merged and resources consolidated. The entire diocese was now to be put on alert – a 'numerically driven-growth-footing'(!) – in which everybody would become an 'equipped disciple enabling transformation'.

My friend was interested in the future maps on display, which showed where the new Hubs would be. He asked, not unreasonably, if the Mission Enabling Team had considered the projected climate change map of the diocese for 2035, which showed fields, rail links, ports, roads and villages under several feet of sea water? Had the Mission Enabling Team thought at all about what kind of world we might be living in 20 years from now? Apparently not.

Recent debates at General Synod demonstrate a church completely out of touch talking as though its finger was on the pulse. Motions 'urge Synod' to improve safeguarding, do more about climate change and condemn the invasion of Ukraine. Synod has no powers or authority to manage any of this. Such proceedings merit little mention in the secular press. Or for that matter, make any impact on the people in the pews worried about where their next vicar will come from, and how to afford the roof repairs for their Grade 1 listed medieval church as well as ever-rising demands for diocesan contributions.

Unlike Noah, the Church of England seems to be in denial, despite the clear indications of likely threats being faced. Were we to conduct a weather forecast for a future of the Church of England, the cultural climate change will have – Canute-like – swamped it within the next 50 years. Already drowning in its own irrelevance, it cannot resist the power of rising cultural tide changes.

That's why whenever I hear most bishops speak these days, I am instantly taken back to Michael Fish's weather report for the BBC on 15 October 1987, just before the Great Storm:

Earlier on today ... a woman rang the BBC and said she heard there was a hurricane on the way; well, if you're watching, don't worry, there isn't ... most of the strong winds will be down over Spain and France.

Memo to bishops: The wind blows where it will. Confident weather forecasts from Church of England bishops cannot change the climate.

The future of establishment

Whether and, if so, how establishment should continue has long been controversial. During the nineteenth century the focus of that discussion turned first on issues of religious *freedom*. Landmarks were Roman Catholic emancipation in 1829, Jewish relief in 1858, Church Tax made voluntary in 1868, the final removal of religious tests at Oxford and Cambridge in 1871, religious tests for burial removed in 1880 and a non-religious affirmation rather than a religious oath permitted from 1888. Disestablishment in Ireland in 1871 and in Wales from 1914 were responses to particular regional circumstances, the latter unfeasible until the removal of the House of Lords legislative veto in 1911.

Modern arguments about disestablishment have centred more on issues of religious *equality* but have also arisen from in-church consideration of the best strategies for survival in an increasingly secular society. Governments themselves have abstained from active participation in public discussion, though their general view is thought to be that these are matters in the first instance for the church itself to decide.

Although such questions were capable of engaging fierce partisan passions in the nineteenth century, the removal of most of the grievances that animated them, and the decline of Christian religious affiliation in the twentieth century, have led to a current situation where they are now little discussed. A 1991 study disclosed that no interviewee spontaneously mentioned the nature of the Queen's relationship with the church. Survey evidence from 2012 suggested that a bare majority favoured retaining establishment – with over a fifth having no view. Ten years on, pro-establishment advocates are far fewer.

Stronger views have, however, been found over whether bishops should remain in the House of Lords. A survey reported in May 2022 showed that whereas a fifth thought they should stay, three-fifths thought they did not have a place in a modern democracy and another fifth were 'don't knows'. Of course, if the Lords were reformed on an elective basis, there would be no place for bishops or any other appointees, religious or not.

The last Royal Commission on the House of Lords thought there was a place for specifically religious representation and would have achieved it by reducing the number of bishops and replacing them with representatives of other religions, recognizing that there were difficulties in identifying appropriate people in the case of non-hierarchical religions. Such solutions may be criticized as reinforcing unacknowledged corporatism, that is, conceding an automatic right of nomination to the nominating body itself. Defence of the present system is difficult when no other democratic assembly has religious representation (apart from the Isle of Man, where the bishop sits by right in the Tynwald, the Parliament).

Some argue that retaining the bishops is crucial for the continuance of the monarchy and that their removal would signify the displacement of religion from public life. The first point seems to be controverted by the fact that the monarchies of Belgium, the Netherlands and Spain have no religious test and no religious parliamentary representation. Religious tests for the monarch survive in Denmark, Norway and Sweden but there is no religious representation in their Parliaments.

A point sometimes made in favour of retention is that bishops have been in Parliament for a very long time. While true, it does not seem to advance the discussion, let alone defeat the observation that the bishops' presence can only be explained as an accidental residue of former constitutional arrangements. Moreover, their removal would not end their ability to make their case publicly on any subject like anyone else. The Church of England would not be removed from the public square but merely asked to take its place there with everyone else. In the interests of equality, the Church of England should surrender the only seats which by a Tudor statute uniquely guarantee a specific place on the overcrowded benches of a bloated assembly, thus offering a much-needed reduction in that assembly's numbers.

The coronation

Coronations do not make a monarch. Under the common law, heirs succeed immediately on the death of the predecessor, and there is therefore no gap in executive rule. Coronations are splendid – and expensive – occasions. Their religious purpose is to signify the descent of God's grace on the ruler and proclaim that the ruler is ultimately answerable to a higher, celestial power.

The UK is the only European monarchy that retains a coronation. Of those countries that had them, coronations ceased in Denmark from 1840, in Sweden from 1873 and in Norway from 1906. Belgium, the Netherlands and (in modern times) Spain have never had them.

In those countries where a monarch is still recognized and symbolically valued, there is a tripartite concord between people, Parliament and head of state. After the investiture of a monarch, a public church service affirming the nation, monarch and people remains commonplace. Ceremonies involve mutual pledges: from people to crown and crown to people. In many European countries the monarch is sworn in or invested by Parliament, and takes an oath to abide by the constitution and defend the laws of the country, and pledges to serve the people, maintain the country's independence and preserve it. Moreover, the new monarch does not take office until the civil as opposed to religious oaths are sworn.

The last UK coronation took place in 1953, some 16 months

after the accession of the Queen. A eucharistic service (according to the 1662 Book of Common Prayer) took almost three hours and crammed 8,200 guests into Westminster Abbey, the largest contingent consisting of hereditary peers (all but 92 of whom are now excluded from Parliament) along with their spouses. The new king Charles let it be understood that he intended his coronation to be swifter, shorter and cheaper than his mother's, though there was no hint that the liturgy would be any different, which struck many in today's radically changed population as incongruently exclusive.

Whether or not the Church of England is disestablished, it is questionable whether there will be another coronation after Charles's. Meanwhile, the present polity of the United Kingdom raises uncomfortable questions for one denomination that seeks to retain its own establishment powers and privilege on behalf of us all. Increasingly, this resembles a kind of 'English Shinto' to many people (which is almost certainly unfair to Shinto). The state at worship – with itself as God's anointed – and like God, English and Anglican?

That said, one of the best things about the Church of England in recent times were the Queen's Christmas broadcasts, who, as head of the Church of England, unfailingly found the right words to capture, lead and inspire the nation at Christmastide, consistently beating into second place any sermon from the Archbishops. She managed to talk to the nations and the world in a way that belied her apparent cocoon. (There is no reason to suppose her heir, Charles III, will be any less able than his mother.) Meanwhile, the Archbishop of Canterbury had to be recently corrected on a small point of self-perception during a visit to Glasgow. No, he is not the spiritual leader of the nation. At least not in Scotland. Or Wales.

If the Church of England is now to be serious about establishment rather than passively assenting and cashing in on the benefits, decisive self-corrective action is needed. These days an unaccountable elite with pretensions to the status of automatic membership of a ruling class, and claiming by implication a rightful, sanctified legitimacy, is probably doomed. Equally, trying to pretend that the United Kingdom and Realms are somehow 'gathered under' one English denomination is in danger of descending into pure theatre. (The one where the emperor has no clothes?)

Canute knew that the monarchy lacked the power to rebuke the winds and the waves. The Church of England needs to read the signs of the times and adapt quickly if it is to survive at all. Rapidly growing indifference towards the Church of England's hierarchy, and its increasing irrelevance to the emerging generation, will not be overcome by tokens of establishment including ceremonies and seats in the House of Lords. Clinging to the privilege and power of the past – in some vain hope of a brand-refreshed, nostalgia-led bounce in numerical growth now that the country has a new monarch – will only see the tides of change rise evermore quickly. Indeed, the evidence is that this cultural climate change has already arrived.

Note

1 A shorter version of this chapter was published in the international journal, *Prospect* (November 2022).

Reflections for Part 3

Do not think that I have come to abolish the Law or the Prophets. I have come not to abolish but to complete. Amen I say to you, till heaven and earth pass away, not one dot, not one little stroke, will pass from the Law until everything is achieved. Therefore, anyone who infringes even one of the least of these commandments and teaches others to do the same will be called least in the kingdom of Heaven; but anyone who keeps them and teaches them will be called great in the kingdom of Heaven. For I tell you, if your righteousness does not surpass that of the scribes and Pharisees, you will never get into the kingdom of Heaven. (Matthew 5.17–20)

According to a published report from some years ago, the Church Commissioners spend around £600,000 per year on cars and drivers for Church of England bishops. Jesus came a lot cheaper. He seemed to walk most places, although he once borrowed a donkey. The Church Commissioners also spend hundreds and thousands of pounds per year on maintaining palaces, castles and other grand residences for bishops. In contrast, 'the Son of Man had nowhere to lay his head': even his tomb belonged to someone else. Jesus wore no mitre; his was the crown of thorns. H. L. Mencken's caustic remark might seem apposite: 'An Archbishop is an ecclesiastic who has attained a rank superior to that of Christ.'

Public interest in bishops and their lifestyles endures for all the right reasons, even if it is wrongly focused. Even in an allegedly secular society, there is a persistent and absorbing inhabiting of holiness. Society still makes room for saints – shining beacons of light, illuminating the darkness. The qualities of such people are to be these: exemplary morals, intense compassion, a degree of asceticism and a life of prayer. In short, a conduit for grace. If a few individuals can live like this, that is some comfort for the millions who believe in God but are tied to more worldly concerns.

For many people, bishops are or should be such people. If clergy are essentially kind and to be trusted, a bishop ought to be much more than this, or so the reasoning goes. They find themselves implicitly pressurized to behave as and be portrayed as the embodiment of the Christian life. As shepherds of God's people, they are meant to be like the Great Shepherd, leading the sheep, and even laying down their lives for them. The burden of expectation is substantial, although the advert simple:

> Messiah Wanted. Managers Need Not Apply. (Fixed-term contract; must be prepared to travel; expenses negotiable; salary details on application; interview dates TBC.)

Stories of expensive cars, chauffeurs and lavish palaces therefore go against the grain for most people. Yet they have their origins in the misunderstandings that surround the office and role of a bishop. In the history of the church, bishops have often been aligned to the prevailing cultures of power. The past has seen bishops, as the leaders of the church, conflated with more secular forms of authority: princes with lands to match, generals in charge of armies, or even feudal lords. Down the centuries, bishops have enjoyed immense power and wealth.

Thankfully, few such trappings survive. Yet bishops still find themselves linked to the normative modes of organizational power that operate in a secular society. Pre-eminent among these is that of the Chief Executive, presiding over other managers, who in turn regulate clergy and laity alike. Given the multifarious demands on bishops today, this is not particularly surprising or scandalous. Running a diocese is a major task, involving several hundred personnel, millions of pounds and massive responsibilities. A good manager at the helm is arguably a better bet than a saint. At least that is the view from the diocesan auditors.

Yet public dis-ease persists. Surely bishops should be the best at prayer, the soundest of pastors, the most spiritual, godly and scholarly of all? Can't the managers manage and leave the ultimate spiritual leadership to the clergy called to that task? It is a simple enough argument, but it ignores the cultural history invested in the office of bishop. Furthermore, it panders to a contemporary culture that often expects too much from individuals and not enough from institutions. This same culture demands saints and gifted leaders who will rule and reign: heroes and icons. Instead of power being dispersed in the church through synods, laity and clergy, it starts to become channelled and concentrated into a single office.

It need not be like this. In the New Testament, a bishop was simply an 'overseer', responsible for an area, a group of churches and their clergy. In such churches, authority was often localized, power shared, and not nearly so much demanded from its leaders. St Paul expressed the simple hope that such people would be 'the husband of but one wife' and 'not given to too much drink'. Management skills are not mentioned.

The Church of England has not added much to this minimalist definition, save to say that a candidate should be 'mature' (over 30 is recommended), be of good character and sound doctrine, and have been a priest for some years. Curiously and somewhat quaintly, they must also be of legitimate birth. Many people would qualify for preferment under these criteria. Patterns of episcopal leadership are always culturally bound, a mixture of tradition, revelation and projection. The real task, then, is to be discerning about which sources are drawn on in the forging of models.

Being a bishop today is an almost impossibly demanding task. In an age where there is an ever-widening gulf between secular and sacred life, bishops frequently find themselves caught in the middle. On the one hand, there is an almost mayoral role to fulfil – a vast range of civic, public and sometimes political duties. On the other, there is the incessant round of confirmations, parochial visits and clerical work. They have to represent the traditional views of the church in order not to alienate their constituencies, who are all too often at each other's throats. At the same time they have to articulate faith and values in a way that is public and inclusive. They do all this only to then get criticized for sitting on the fence. Actually, this is probably the only place to be, given that they are also supposed to be a figure symbolizing unity.

The demanding double-bind of diplomacy coupled to directionality is not easy. The provision of leadership while keeping the peace is certainly tricky. Being prophetic while providing pastoral oversight is almost incompatible. Bishops have to call the church to take risks, but also to play it safe; to go forward, yet respect the past. It is a task that any potential leader might be wary of. Yet that is precisely where the rhetoric of careers and management gives way to that of service and vocation. Emma Percy's poem, 'Humbled', counsels wisely:

When you are brought low
When you are humbled
When you are ground down
And hit rock bottom
Humble yourself
Feel the solidity of the earth
Become grounded

Then when you know who you are
Hold firm to the rock
Feel its strength
Clamber up
And find your feet.
Raise your head and
Carefully, tentatively
Walk forward
With a new perspective

A new understanding
A new joy in living.

St Augustine was a reluctant celibate and an even more reluctant bishop. More than most, he understood how corrupting power could be, especially in the episcopacy: 'For you, I am a bishop, with you, after all, I am a Christian. The first is the name of an office undertaken, the second a name of grace; that one means danger, this one salvation.' That, quite simply, is the See of Faith. Augustine's 'On the Anniversary of His Ordination' (Sermon 340) provides a beautiful portrait of pastoral ministry (*The Works of Saint Augustine*, 1990, pp. 292–4).

Discussion

Scan the advertisement sections of your denominational newspaper – *Church Times, Church of England Newspaper, Methodist Recorder*, etc. – and pick at random 20 announcements, calls or commercials inviting a new pastor, priest or minister. Make a list of the requirements and most frequently used words in the advertisements, and then list separately those that you'd expect or hope for but don't appear.

- What is being asked of the person who is to apply (skills, beliefs, energies, passions, etc.)? What do these advertisements express about the wider church and the local congregation?
- What virtues and charisms are missing from these advertisements?
- What do you want from your bishop, minister, vicar or clergy?

PART 4

Rickety Religion

9

Issues

So, to our first question: what is the Church of England called to be? I have a hunch that Pope Francis gave us an important clue to one core proposition, when in an audience in late August 2019 he opined that the early church was often depicted as 'a field hospital that takes in the weakest people ... it is for the infirm'.

> 'The sick hold a privileged role in the Church,' said Pope Francis. He added, 'they are not to be cast aside ... on the contrary, they are to be cared for, to be looked after [for] they are the focus of our Christian concern.' A humble national church will be a field hospital for everyone – a pop-up spiritual NHS service for all citizens. It will be rickety in part, but resolute in others. It will not seek to dominate, for it is here to serve. Service – after the example of Jesus – is what it must do and be. It is local and lowly. (Martyn Percy, *The Humble Church*, 2021)

The Anglican theologian Daniel Wayne Hardy used to speak of the responsibility of the church to be the 'social skin' of the community or nation it served. In other words, to be an embodied and incarnational expression of Christ for the world in the context in which it was called to be. 'Social skin' is a telling phrase because it implies something vulnerable, undefended and even exposed. This has little to do with the well-padded, armour-plated Teflon church variety that is so well protected and insulated and that we have become rather accustomed to. Skin, rather, implies reception and reaction. We feel the cold of the homeless on a winter night. We feel the pain of the victims of violence and abuse. We sense the soreness and scarring in our communities that may have come from wounds, accidents or blows struck long ago. We are conscious of our colour, and what that says about us. We bruise easily. We can be pierced. We bleed. But we can be warm, tender, affectionate; sensing, feeling and swaddling. We live in our skin.

There is a frequent Christian claim that says we don't choose to change (e.g., Cain in the Old Testament and Paul in the New Testament come to mind), and sometimes it is only by being humbled – reputationally, morally, intellectually, spiritually, physically and psychologically – that we find God's surgery of the soul within us can begin. But there is a close relationship between humbling ourselves and our humiliation. Sometimes humiliation creates the ground for humility; it is the necessary preface.

The Apostle Paul, who saw everything so clearly as a zealot (yet in black-and-white terms), had to be (literally) blinded by the light. It was only through the cracks in his zeal that the light and truth penetrated and he began to see God's world in other colours: the gospel is for Gentiles, slaves and foreigners; women can lead in churches and society, and be equally valued and regarded, just as the male leaders always assumed was their God-given birthright; refraining from certain foods, circumcision and other customs could not make God love you more than others, or any less, because God has no grandchildren.

If we want to be the children of God, we can be adopted in Christ, and learn and wean from him. But we cannot pass this on through inheritance. Deep down we know that to resist the work of God – the endless reconstruction of ourselves in the imago Dei – is something we cannot contribute much towards, save our assent ('yes') and suppleness ('let it be to me according to his word'). Without yielding to God, we will not experience true grace, illumination and transformation. We will, instead, invest our energies in being what God has *not* called us to be: self-sufficient, self-reliant and self-perpetuating.

Sometimes accepting God's demolition of us, and the possibility of a complete reconstruction, is better than preservation, conservation, repair and resistance to God's work. Our besetting sin in the church – with us for well over two centuries and more – is our buy-in to endless models, visions and programmes of self-help and self-improvement. But first and foremost, God wants us with as little baggage as possible. The less there is, the more God can do with it. Loaves and fish are just one illustration. Likewise, the first disciples. Oh, and the early church. Christian faith is partly about casting aside all that binds us and beginning to follow the light to the distant glow of a stable in an otherwise forgettable rural village in some far-flung occupied territory. A completely pointless place of pilgrimage: a waste of time being there. Such is God; his work of renewal and redemption begins in the wasteland of a vast mighty empire. Our besetting sins recall the first sin, and our attempts to cover it up should make us wince.

Adam and Eve give us a familiar paradigm for individuals and institutions. Thinking they might know more than God, they succumb to temptation. Blame is passed around, and no one takes responsibility. In a vain effort to cover their shame, they sew fig leaves together to cover their sense of disgrace and nakedness. If you ever want to run a Bible study on the early chapters of Genesis, a compelling exercise for attendees is to give them a needle and thread and some fig leaves, and see what they come up with. It is futile and very funny. For this is midrash – a kind of espresso shot of dark humour. Only when Adam and Eve are expelled from the Garden of Eden do they get to wear proper clothes – and even these are made and tailored by God from animal skins. The fig leaves are not mentioned again.

The first sin is contempt: God need not be relied upon, or even trusted; we could do better if we helped ourselves a bit more and depended upon God a little less; God might think our self-motivated attempts at self-improvement would not amount to a breach of covenant; we could blame a third party (a serpent) for our hubris, or blame each other (s/he made me do it). The fear of the Lord is the beginning of wisdom. When we lose that humility, foolishness finds a home. A ready one too, with vacant possession – for wisdom has been evicted.

Contempt is a step towards self-destruction, and institutions that have the contagion are mostly destroyed from the inside out. The tipping point will just be the proverbial straw that breaks the camel's back; the one extra snowflake that made the roof cave in. So if the first sin was contempt, what are we asked to recall? Several things come to mind, but here are three brief propositions.

First, there is a very real difference between contempt and dissent. Indeed, loyal dissent is important for institutions and is to be encouraged and valued. Institutions deal in established norms, patterns and paradigms for behavioural relations that express good values and practices.

Second, institutions are, for the most part, free (or very heavily subsidized at their point of delivery, though some are paid-for and private, and universities and colleges vary hugely). As services, they also rest on largely voluntary and free associations that bond us by shared values and commitments, and do not oblige us by contract. Institutions can rarely compel and will be limited in what they can enforce. Yet they are essential in a civil society and they primarily lead by example. As such, they cannot afford to be held in contempt by those they serve; nor do they treat those they serve with contempt.

Third, and in that memorable sociological phrase 'structure is an expression of value' (see Clegg, *The Theory of Power and Organizations*, 1979; Gerlach and Hine, *People, Power, Change*, 1970; and Martyn Percy, *Words, Wonders and Power*, 1996, pp. 116–19), our institutions sometimes need to look at themselves carefully in the mirror and reflect on how their very structured-ness sends out signals and signposts as to what is valued and cherished. It is perhaps for this reason that the birth of Jesus is – according to tradition, at least – in a rickety town, in a rickety stable and in a rickety crib. There is something here about permanence, reliability and stability that God seems to have bypassed. Quite deliberately.

We live in an age that has been weaned on stability, predictability and reliability. Covid-19 and its variants have knocked our self-assurance. Our self-directed teleology has been tampered with and we no longer quite know how this will all end. Our confidence has been quietly shattered by the turmoil and lack of trust in politics and international relations, the trials and tribulations of our migrants and refugees, and the uncertainty of climate change and other ecological disasters. It is in such uncertain and unstable times that churches need to remember that they too are subject to these forces.

Churches are not meant to exist in order to withstand such challenges and remain aloof from them. Rather, we are to be the field hospitals of every age, pitching our tents where they are most needed for those who are most vulnerable. Only to be great for those who are least. Our calling is one of risk and responsibility for those who have nothing. The kingdom of God was first practised and proclaimed by a bunch of ragamuffin disciples and their itinerant rabbi-leader. It was a precarious venture that went where the needs of others took them. There was little sign of a plan, strategy or campaign. The task was to be the love of God wherever they found themselves.

Our calling begins with a rickety, roughshod prophet in the wilderness, proclaiming the coming of one who is greater than he. It continues with a young woman, chosen to bear a child, yet to be part of a stable and committed relationship. All in a village, with few prospects, and little in the way of support on offer to an unmarried mother. These are the precarious, rickety beginnings for Jesus.

So let us cast aside all the works within our denominations that prevent us from embracing that precarious church and rickety religion we were called to inhabit and embody. Sometimes less is so much more. It is where Jesus begins his life and will later continue in his ministry. Remember the rickety, precarious places – the where, with whom and in what Jesus abides. Be there.

10

Structures

We begin by inviting you to enter this perfectly ordinary scenario within the Church of England. This is a gathering of the Bishop's Council, and you need to imagine a medium-sized facility, out of town, situated on a campus estate of other offices and regional headquarters. Inside this diocesan Church House there are committee rooms, offices and some larger conference spaces. Bishop's Council is held in the largest of these rooms, with a sizeable boardroom table around which members gather, with officers and secretaries sitting along the sides. So far, so good. The composition of those seated around the table, at first sight, looks encouraging. While it is only 25 per cent female and 75 per cent male, this is better than it was a few years ago. In terms of age, the youngest will be over 40 and the oldest north of 60. The facial complexions are overwhelmingly white, but we have two exceptions to that in the room. This is, again, better than it was a few years ago. There is wheelchair access to this ground-floor room and, as it happens, one member of the Council has got mobility issues that require this gathering to be accessible.

This Council is fairly satisfied that this is a 'balanced' representation of the diocese. Yet appearances can be deceptive. Two of the women and one of the men seated at the table are there to represent the interests of those churches who oppose women being ordained as priests or bishops. This is assumed to be balanced because everyone else accepts women clergy. However, only one woman at the table will ever vocally speak up for equality. The Bishop's Adviser on Women in Ministry post was phased out long ago, once women could become bishops. That, it seems, put an end to any gender-based discrimination, so no further advocacy was needed. There is one person at the table who is gay, has a steady partner and has entered into a civil partnership. To keep the balance, there are two people also at the table who represent those churches that oppose equal marriage and think that gay clergy should not be permitted in the church. Those churches campaign on such matters and, for reasons of conscience, withhold much of their quota payments from the diocese. Yet they need a seat at the table too, so they can continue to express their position. You see, it is important to maintain that sense of balance.

We don't know what people around the table think about disability or ethnicity. All persons in the room are sufficiently self-aware to know that you cannot discriminate against people on grounds of ethnicity or disability. That would be wrong, and illegal. But sexuality and gender are different, are they not? Nobody in the room has ever had the chutzpah to say that this would have been the same 150 years ago, when slavery was permitted in some parts of the worldwide Anglican church. Or that discrimination on grounds of race was tolerated and sanctioned by some churches until quite recently – our lifetime, in fact. Nothing is said, because we have all been educated into accepting opt-outs on equality regarding gender and sexuality and schooled not to compare such stances to ethnicity or other aspects of human identity. And this board meeting aspires to be representative and balanced.

As the Council gathers, it looks, to all intents and purposes, like any executive board meeting might in any other commercial organization. The bishop sits at the head, flanked by advisers and assistants. To begin the meeting, today's Bible study is about equality, mutuality, service and vocation. Nobody notes the irony. That the room comprises persons who would deny the right of others present to be there is part of the balance that is being maintained. That the chairing of this is usually done by a white male is barely referenced. In any case, he will be at pains to point out that the balance means none should be excluded and that all minorities must be affirmed. Here, women find themselves referenced in peculiar sentences that usually group them together with other minorities worthy of representation and inclusion.

This scenario is pretty typical for many a diocese, and I dare say other versions of it exist in PCCs, chapters and synods across the land. But perhaps what is striking about the specifics of the scenario above are the things we now take for granted, so much so that they strike us as neither strange nor peculiar. Yet, I think the scene set is much stranger than you might think, and would have puzzled and perplexed almost all bishops in the Church of England up to 1950.

But why? Here are five brief suggestions. First, why is the diocesan HQ in this location, why are so many people staffing it, and what do they spend their days doing? To be sure, there is HR, stewardship, mission, evangelism, social responsibility, overseas mission links, ever-growing panoplies of communication and safeguarding staff, education, clergy housing, the diocesan newspaper, IT, offices for archdeacons and others, and more besides. The annual running costs are drawn from the quota extracted from parishes, which in turn is set by those occupying diocesan HQ, overseeing their various growing service levels and ministries that need to be provided for.

Second, you can begin to see why this might puzzle and perplex. After all, who would ever ring up or call in on the diocesan HQ (located in a largely forgettable campus of light-industrial buildings and low-rise office blocks) and ask for a baptism, wedding or funeral? Or just a pastoral visit? Few would know where this HQ was or what it was for. For 99.9 per cent of the population, the Church of England is to be found in the parish church, meeting hall, vicarage or chaplaincy. Indeed, for 99.9 per cent of people on the electoral rolls of any diocese, a visit to central HQ will never be necessary or ever happen. I mean, why would you?

Third, we are struck by how similar the diocesan HQ building and the operation of staff are to the neighbouring businesses. Boardrooms, meeting rooms, open-plan working, offices and the like. When and how did the business of the church start to look so similar to other kinds of business? I don't say that this is right or wrong. But the resemblances would strike our predecessors as being peculiar. And perhaps unsettling?

Fourth, if you were given a tour of diocesan HQ, you might be surprised to learn that 25 per cent of the entire diocesan staffing budget (covering all of the clergy stipends, housing, allowances and other support) was consumed by this operation, located somewhere on the edge of town with other company HQs. They would be even more surprised to learn that for every £1 a parish raises, 75 per cent goes directly to the diocese to meet 'central costs'. True, parishes and chaplaincy continue to be affirmed as 'front-line mission'. But it is a peculiar front line if 75 per cent of the resources are immediately sent back to HQ, many, many miles away from the real action. An army doing this would not fare well.

Fifth, although past bishops such as Edward White Benson (1829–96) and Edward King (1829–1910) could not have been immersed in sociology, they might have wondered at the relationship between the headquarters and the branches, or the central office and the local outlets. As we noted in the first part of these reflections, that memorable sociological phrase 'structure is an expression of value' (see Stewart Clegg, *The Theory of Power and Organizations*, 1979; and Martyn Percy, *Words, Wonders and Power*, 1996, pp. 116–19) leads us to ask if churches need to reflect more on how their structuring signposts what really matters; the indispensable and valued. Benson and King would undoubtedly be perturbed by the growth of the central HQ, and the cuts made on the front line. They'd ask, surely, 'If the Church of England is primarily known through its local interfacing – parish clergy and chaplains – what are we doing cutting those posts and putting more money into a centre that nobody sees or would ever really care for, let alone visit? What are we valuing, exactly?'

You get the drift here. There is not much point in the Royal Mail if you close half of the local Post Offices and cull tens of thousands of post boxes. 'A presence in every community' is a fine marketing tag-line for the Church of England, but such sentiments become less plausible and trustworthy if the local outlets get absorbed into much larger districts, which in turn collapse into being regional hubs. Of course, we can do some things online. But no central HQ can afford to keep growing at the expense of the local presence in the community. The identity and value of the Royal Mail is tied up in its local accessibility, familiarity and availability. The Post Office parable for the Church of England needs little exposition. Like churches, every Post Office is different. They bumble along providing a reassuring level of service, and serve us, as institutions do, with many of the basics that communities need to keep themselves open and connected.

Yet somehow, bishops, diocesan HQs and their staff have come to resemble a small-to-medium-sized franchise operation. They govern their branches remotely, set them targets and channel their latest offerings and products through the local staff. The diocese has a new vision, plan, needs or message – and the outlet is required to market this, and pay central HQ for continuing to be a staffed outlet. But beware, if the outlet misses its target, it is in danger of losing its staffing and ultimately risks closure. This is a strange business model for the church, a kind of ecclesiocracy that is based on ecclesionomics. Yet, oddly, this is an organization that is cutting back on the outlets locally in order to concentrate on its regional branding. In most of our light-industrial out-of-town office complexes, the lights go out at roughly 6 p.m. and the car park will empty. It becomes a wilderness where no one will hear you scream.

Bishop John Robinson once opined that the House of God is 'primarily the world in which God lives, not the contractor's hut set up in the grounds' (Robinson, *The New Reformation*, 1965, p. 27). The church was only ever meant to be the Constructor's Hut on God's Building Site, which is the world. I think Robinson – not to mention Benson and King – would have been perplexed to find these huts closing, and one giant regional shiny HQ hub being developed and staffed in place of the business of building the kingdom of God in our local communities. Structure, remember, is an expression of value.

Of course, the church is not God's primary preoccupation, and a diocesan HQ even less so. The world is God's main concern. Jesus thought so too, and acted accordingly, and died and rose again for this very reason. Helping to bring about the kingdom of God is Christian faith. We are not called to be devoted members of the Diocesan Preservation Society (excellent work though such bodies undoubtedly do). For Christians, Jesus is the body language of God. He sees the unseen, hears the unheard, speaks for the mute and marginalized, touches the untouchable. The incarnation reconciled the gap between humanity and divinity.

Hortense Calisher once observed that 'sociology functions best by alarm'. In some respects, it is only possible to blow on the glowing embers of concern by judicious use of sociological parallels. Zygmunt Bauman once noted that 'The task of sociology is to come to the help of the individual. We have to be in the service of freedom.' The service of freedom can come through macro-scale institutions (that is, religion, family units in general, the law, universities, etc.), meso-scale subgroups (such as judges, bishops, vice-chancellors, etc.); and finally, micro-scale actions (that is, the local, familial, ordinary or intimate business of everyday living, etc.). We need kindness, truth and service to permeate the macro, meso and micro at every level. But nothing is gained – and all may be lost – if the leadership groups occupying the meso level do not understand the macro scale, and no longer value the micro levels of institutional life. Increasingly, however, dioceses find themselves being restructured, overmanaged and overpowered at the micro and macro levels by hubristic meso-level managers and their blueprints for change. Left unchecked, this will only cause catastrophic long-term damage to the identity, mission and value of the church in local communities and chaplaincies.

Yet there seems to be no end to flow charts, mission action plans, strategies, targets and reviews, and all those other forms of 'soft bullying' now so prevalent in the 'disciplining' (usually called 'discipling') of clergy and congregations into deferring to the greater powers and growing needs of middle management, who dominate the rest from their meso-level platform. (Benson and King might ask, 'Do you really need all of this? We managed for a long time without diocesan HQs; we can probably cope without them now ...') The other problem underlying the present restructuring of the Church of England is that it became easy prey to the late-capitalist rhetoric of growth-related metrics, returns, conglomeration and rationalization. This is fine for businesses that are running a franchise operation, or perhaps resourcing and stocking outlets. But it is a hopeless, hapless foundation for institutions, and perhaps especially churches.

We are called to be in the places nobody wants to be and to richly abide among those people and communities that nobody wants to be with. Institutions have two primary functions: socialization and stabilization. The extended family is perhaps the smallest and oldest form of institution known to humanity, and it is no accident that the earliest churches were based on such units: the *oikos* (household) of faith, comprising old, young, widows, paid and slave labour, freeborn, kith and kin. The early churches understood that you could not run Corinth out of Galatia or manage Philippi from Thessalonica. These people and places needed various kinds of visits and letters from Paul because they had their own local issues to resolve. Each one needed a different kind of empathy, compassion, attention and direction. Their office was wherever they were.

The New Testament does not give us a 'General Epistle to People in General'. That's why the first bishops were so mobile. They could not sit in offices and run things from some centre. Paul would have agreed with Graham Greene: 'One can't love humanity. One can only love people.' Likewise, there is no 'general ministry' for 'these people generally'. It is always local, particular and free. That is what makes ministry so expansive, expensive, exhausting ... and exhilarating. These are some of the reasons to restructure the resourcing of the church for local service and move away from centralization. Such things belong to the world of business and, while we can learn from these, we have no need to replicate them. Our whole business model is different.

11

Time and Place

Sociologists claim that institutions have two primary functions: socialization and stabilization. We are called to be in the places nobody wants to be, and to richly abide among those people and communities that nobody wants to be with. Now, every family needs some organization. But it is particular, seasonal, time-specific, adaptable, organic, reciprocal and humane. No family is organized like a commercial company or industry. Families have values, and as we are raised with these, so we may have the opportunity to replicate or reform them as we age. Marriages and their ancient predecessors are similar – again, they all require an adaptability, stability and selflessness to thrive. Marriages, like families, need love, honesty, integrity, patience, kindness, self-control, humility, gentleness and faithfulness.

As the previous chapter invited us into an opening scenario, we continue with another here. I want you to imagine the exercise of an annual spousal appraisal. These were introduced for good reasons, not least to see if they might provide a mechanism to check rising rates of separation and divorce. So, a good thing? Maybe. In our imagined scenario, a spouse hands the form over to their partner to be filled in. There are questions to answer, such as, 'How have you grown and developed this year?', 'What extra training have you done?', 'Have you read anything helpful to you in your spousal role?', 'Have you met the goals and targets from last year?' (last year's appraisal form enclosed), and 'Did you manage to get away for a break to refresh your sense of purpose in this relationship?' The partner may find this exercise a tad trivializing, but there is an opportunity to expand on your responses. In one box on the form, you are asked to write in not less than 300 words how your vision for this relationship is being worked through. Another box asks you to write down what has been challenging this year. There are more boxes to indicate extra training or support you might want to make the relationship even better. Your continuous improvement as a spouse is such a given that there is no need to question the setting of goals and any means of achieving them. Why would you not want to improve?

To help this exercise be more effective, the architect of the appraisal scheme recommends you invite some other spouses in from your neighbourhood, and other members of your household, to comment on your performance. This is explained as 'good practice'. Because we can always learn from the insights of others, and if we are to grow in our roles, then we should be open to constructive criticism and how others see us. There is no need to worry about the confidentiality of this process – the form is filled in, signed and then returned to those in authority who can discuss this with you later. It is pointed out to you that appraisals are helpful in all other work-related roles, and any objections you have to this being an annual process are unreasonable 'because this is standard practice in all other places'.

While I accept that this kind of annual exercise might take quite a dark turn – *Stepford Wives* or *The Handmaid's Tale* come to mind – the parallel is intentionally comedic. Who in their right mind would not see the functionality and triviality of this exercise as something to be resisted and rejected? How could it *not* be demeaning of the persons in role? And yet those in religious orders or ordained – at least in Catholic and Orthodox traditions – will see themselves as 'married' to the church. Even in ordinary parlance within the Church of England, how many wives, husbands and partners speak of the parish as being 'the other man/woman in the Vicar's life'?

In ministry, we often experience ourselves as being married to or engaged in the parenting of the parish and congregation. The New Testament, moreover, provides plenty of references to and images of filial, parental, household and marital motifs to help us identify the role of the minister in relation to those s/he cares for, loves and cherishes. Fathers or mothers in God (bishops) is hardly casual terminology. It is not uncommon to refer to other clergy in the same way. I am not sure what an appraisal of my parenting would look like, or where to begin to assess my 'performance' as a husband in an annual appraisal. As a minimum, I would hope to be valued, loved, appreciated and respected. However, I am not sure how I would respond to the box asking me to specify targets and goals for next year, and what would happen if I didn't meet them. I guess it depends on what else life had in store. I mean, if I suffered a serious bereavement or health-related problem, would my spousal targets be adjusted? Would they even matter? Who decides?

Well, so much for the annual spousal appraisal. Although when I did suggest this exercise to a cathedral chapter quite recently, most chuckled (uncontrollably), a few said they thought it might not be a bad idea (if they were doing the appraising), and one much older gentleman informed us all that he had been subject to such daily appraisal for much of his married life.

Behind this wry remark, however, there was a serious point: how do we reflect upon *any* of our relational roles in life? And, of course, many clergy come to rue a moment when they discover they were only as good as their last sermon or most recent pastoral visit. They are never good enough, and live in a constant state of scrutiny, judgement and inchoate appraisal. There will always be some in the parish or congregation who believe they could be better. It is hard for clergy to be 'engaged' in such committed relationships. The last thing they need from their bishop is another appraisal. Some care and love would be better; ideally some empathy and compassion. (I dare to live in hope.)

Annual clergy appraisals were introduced many moons ago and they are part and parcel of an exceedingly long game. As the Church of England struggles to explain itself as a public, transparent and accountable utility in the modern world, it resorts to – 'magpie-like' – picking up shiny concepts and phrases that it thinks will make it look like other kinds of organization. It does so in the hope that if the world recognizes the currency of these concepts and terms generally, the church will be less 'other' and remain accessible and perhaps maintain its plausibility. Of course, this does not work. Not for a moment. For a start, the things the magpie-like church picks up tend to have been cast away ages ago. I recall reading extracts of the Green report to a gathering of university business school lecturers and professors (*Talent Management for Future Leaders and Leadership Development for Bishops and Deans*, 2014). After the first paragraph – read, I might add, sincerely – the audience began to chuckle, and by the time I'd read the third extract, they were laughing. They saw immediately that the language of the report was out of date by about 25 years. Likewise, in another similar gathering in a different university, there was a similar reaction to the language of vision, strategy, aims, objectives, outcomes, SMART targets and other metrics (SMART is an acronym that stands for Specific, Measurable, Achievable, Realistic and Timely). Both audiences were uncomprehending of the church at these points, and on two counts: first, the dated concepts in use, which academics and practitioners had set aside decades ago; second, how, in any case, could such concepts ever be a 'fit' for an institution such as the church? They simply weren't applicable.

I have long held the view that clergy do not have *work* to do. When they are classed as part-time, full-time, stipendiary or non-stipendiary minister (NSM) we are placing them in a category that is comparable to mother, father, parent, spouse, partner. Are you a part-time spouse? Can you ever be a full-time parent? What does that even mean? (This is explored in significant and rich depth in Emma Percy's *Mothering as Metaphor for Ministry* (2014), and *What Clergy Do: Especially When It Looks Like Nothing* (2015).) Can there be any 'time' when you are not in these relational roles? The words 'part', 'full' and 'non' surely relate to contracts, money and other employment, but they have little to do with your role. For this and other reasons, I have argued that clergy, like some other roles, are better thought of as an 'occupation' than as a job, or even as a profession. Being clergy is not a 'profession' in the conventional, work-related sense of the term. True, it involves the profession of faith in word and deed, and in life and limb.

It becomes quickly apparent on a rudimentary, comparative basis that the role of clergy is not a profession in the way that a doctor, dentist or solicitor might be. No one checks in for an appointment with their non-stipendiary dentist or sees a doctor who only practises at weekends as they have a different job during the week. Nobody instructs a solicitor who lacks the relevant academic or professional qualifications. To be ordained, it is desirable, but not mandatory, to have a degree or other theological qualification. Nor do you need to have passed an exam or be qualified in the way that other workers would be for their profession. Clergy, in this regard, are more like poets, writers and artists. It is hard to say what a 'productive day' consists of. Their work is creative, never-ending, tidal and seasonal. It depends on a spirit of generative good will.

The nature of this occupation to which clergy are bound is threefold. First, to be occupied with God. Second, to be as preoccupied as you can be with what you think might occupy God's heart and mind. Third, be an occupant, as Christ was, in the world; he 'dwelt among us' – to abide with people in a particular time and place, and in a way that manifests the love and grace of God drawing near to those who are far off, lost, lonely or in need. I have yet to see a clergy appraisal form that appears to understand what clergy are for, and what they 'do'. In most cases, if not all, the role of clergy has been completely misconceived as a set of functional tasks and targets that belong to the world of work. They have little to do with prayer, abiding, caring, nourishing and cherishing. The work of a parent, to some extent – a role that can, some days, be rewarding and other days thankless. Clergy, like parents, are dependent on the behaviour, maturing and respect that those they care for might return to them. And if they receive no such tokens, they cannot dismiss their children or congregation, or put them on probation, with a view to a process of redundancy or even firing them. No. They have to love them through this. Sometimes for a long season. Sometimes for several seasons.

You can begin to see why bishops have become so tempted by the grammar of appraisals, reviews, discipline, permission to officiate and licensing. It is the antidote to their helplessness; it bypasses their need to be patient and to care for the clergy and the congregations under them. If insistence does not work, the gears move swiftly through admonition and review processes, until we get to something close to a take-it-or-leave-it exit interview. None of this culture can ever read or respect the vocational life, with all its ambivalence. Soft bullying is quickly re-narrated into 'pastoral reorganization'. If you are hurt or crushed by that, you can have 'pastoral care' – but let there be no doubt about what that consists of: it will not involve advocacy. Sympathy, yes, empathy too, and perhaps compassion, but not any support in refusing the changes being imposed.

In Kenneth Thompson's *Bureaucracy and Church Reform: The Organizational Response of the Church of England to Social Change, 1880–1965* (1970), he argues that the church has been moved around on some very significant cultural tectonic plates in the wake of the Industrial Revolution. The relationship between church, land and locality has been fundamentally disrupted. The Church of England responded to the huge changes in urbanization and migration (the population of England was 75 per cent rural, and in the space of 50 years became 75 per cent urban and inner city). New churches were built to cope with the population flux and tried to establish themselves (imposing their taxation rate upon the locals) in these new emergent cities. In many cases, the new churches were unwelcome.

The Church of England responded to this alienation with more organization and differentiation as they became more specialized and delimited in their functions. Frenetic organizational activism was one way to achieve self-validation and hopefully achieve public recognition. But frenetic organizational activism rarely attracts the public as a whole, though it will, for a season, increase membership. These changes all led to highly rationalized bureaucracies being formed, and ideologies that supported their legitimization quickly came into being. In practical terms, this meant the Church of England as an 'institution' slowly shifted towards becoming a smaller, more rationalized and measurable 'organization'. In turn, our bishops have been drawn to the cultural movement from the leadership of institutions into the management of organizations.

Christian faith always invites us to reflect on time and on what matters – what can be cast away and what is now to be taken on. Increasingly, it is becoming clearer that what the Church of England has taken on over the course of the last two centuries is less than conducive for its health and identity. The magpie mentality has not served us well. We are in a new century and a new cultural season, where imitating the world of work and business no longer grants us public plausibility – if indeed it ever did. It is time to get back to basics. We could hardly do better than ask, 'What kind of body does God ask the Church of England to be for the nation and in our communities, and for whom are our clergy, churches and chaplaincies?' Our best answers will certainly involve less power and resources gravitating towards some remote HQ and return to comprehending that the Church of England (and God!) are experienced most truly when alive in the local. Bishops will always be most welcome to visit such places, time permitting.

12

Post-Structuralism

One general approach to writing job specifications is to set out what one might require from candidates applying for the post. What are the essential qualities, skills and experience a candidate needs? What are the desirable ones, but, if necessary, those the organization or institution could manage without? Assuming, that is, that they find a candidate that wants the post and meets all the essential criteria. Now, suppose for a moment the tables are turned and the candidates approach each vacancy with the same list. As they do not need this new post, they can afford to browse and probe the interviewers searchingly for responses and answers that satisfy the interviewee that their own essential and desirable criteria are addressed.

Most of us don't tend to approach job interviews like this – at least not consciously. Yet to do so, in part, might help us understand a bit more about the deeper synergies that underpin workers and their workplaces. Imagine now, by extension, we ask parishioners and church members to say what they want from their parish church. Parishioners in most places, or places with chaplains serving the workforce, if an opinion is expressed, will typically want their clergy to be accessible and for the ministry to be kind, pastoral and authentic. They will want comfort, care and compassion. And yes, a Christian faith and ministry that serves others, speaks for those who have no voice, and is extensive in its outlook. Comfortable pews and good coffee at the end of a service are desirable, but not essential. Good and truthful clergy are essential, not desirable. Church members, in contrast, might see things slightly differently, and expect and hope for a ministry that is less extensive and focused much more on the intensive.

We can sympathize with this. After all, 'members' are the committed ones, and in that commitment have reasonable expectations of their intensive concerns being met and addressed, rather than seeing their resources, labour, time, clergy and pastors dissipated through seemingly endless extensity.

The Gospels, early church and New Testament paint a picture of the extensive and the intensive together. Often the two are held in tension, which can be a creative harmony but sometimes prompts serious disagreement. Is this the time to withdraw from the crowds and pray alone, seeking the face of God? Yes. However, the crowds don't have much time for disciples developing their spiritual intensity. This crowd is needy right now, and they did not walk miles so that the disciples could simply slip away on some private retreat. As all clergy know, you cannot win on this one. Ministry, of course, is not a game, and so there are no winners. Ministry is not a competition with prizes to be handed out in various categories.

(Brief interlude – firmest handshake in the Deanery; most reassuring, upper-middle-class modulated preaching voice [sub-category: male, evangelical]; do add your own ...) Ministry is demanding, 24/7, perpetual, unending, seasonal, strenuous, wearing, exciting, exhilarating – and exhausting. Think: slow rollercoaster, but without health-and-safety audits.

So, the puzzle we have before us is this. How has the centralization of services offered by any diocesan HQ – the centralization of powers and permissions – been allowed to grow at such a steady and growing rate in the post-war era? It is not unfair to characterize the Church of England in the post-war years as having moved from being over-led and under-managed to being over-bureaucratized and under-led. Kenneth Thompson addressed this in *Bureaucracy and Church Reform: The Organizational Response of the Church of England to Social Change – 1880–1965* (1970).

Yet for most clergy, the new shapes of the Church of England have simply produced slow, rising levels of anxiety and disenchantment. Moreover, as the managerial-bureaucratic centralization is resisted and rejected – by all wings and quarters of the Church of England – this only causes the church to search for even stronger forms of management, together with rationalizing and efficiencies that will deliver reinvigorated public recognition. (Clergy appraisals, discussed in chapter 11, are part of this. Likewise, the Church of England's 'Core Groups' in safeguarding, which bear no resemblance to their social-work counterparts.) The key question is this: what is essential in a diocese, and what is (merely) desirable? If you'd asked this question of the Church of England in the first half of the twentieth century, there would be little to place in the 'essential' category. Other than a bishop (probably only one per diocese, mostly) to be available to talk to and care for the clergy, and regularly visit the parishes. A bishop to speak for the region when needed (public theology and social advocacy). A bishop to ordain, confirm and baptize. There might be a chaplain to keep the bishop in order, and possibly a secretary to handle correspondence and communications. (Both of these, arguably, were desirable, not essential.) There would be a registrar for legal services, and a chancellor to manage the seasonal spats on church re-orderings and graveyards.

Most dioceses in the Anglican Communion get by with this infrastructure, with some provinces managing with less. The Church of England managed for more than a few hundred years like this. So the infrastructure today is puzzling and would confound Archbishop Benson and Bishop King. It would baffle Bishop George Bell and Archbishop William Temple. Now, I don't want to suggest for a moment that we could manage as they once did. The world has changed. The nation is different, and culture transformed. So, let me add some new 'essentials' to the brief list above.

First, I think HR is a growing need in churches and parishes. Whether parochial staff are paid or unpaid, many issues of congregational intra-relations now require HR counsel: choirs that fall out with clergy and congregations; or bellringers, youth leaders and more besides. Clergy and PCCs rarely have

HR expertise. A diocese could provide it. It is astonishing that most dioceses provide no HR counsel to their own clergy and PCCs as they struggle with their own local legal and personnel issues. It would make an enormous difference if the dioceses did help.

Second, following the example of the dozen or so major mainline denominations in the USA, most of their national offices are staffed with officers (several) who are skilled in mediation, conflict resolution and the pastoral care of congregations impacted by grief, trauma or catastrophe. In some cases, these officers can spend months or even a few years walking alongside the congregation or parish while it recovers. Routinely, the presence of such officers is premised on them not being a candidate for any clergy vacancy. Like a good doctor (for the cure of the bruised collective soul), they come with healing balm, care, compassion, experience and empathy. The patient is treated and the doctor moves on.

Third, there is a clear need for national and local diocesan advocacy, support and therapy services. The offer of 'pastoral care' is always appreciated, but many issues faced by clergy cannot be addressed by this. Pastoral care without advocacy will be ineffective in the face of systemic racism, sexism, bullying, discrimination and other forms of serious and long-term contextual conflict. Pastoral care is not a panacea, and if we treat it as such we relegate 'cure-alls' to being a placebo. Clergy and congregations need remedies that are effective, and this means dioceses being much more serious about the conditions of being clergy – a paid coordinator of an entirely voluntary body – but where there are no contracts to bind or oblige the volunteers.

This then leaves us with what might be 'desirable' for the infrastructure of a modern diocese. Although by this I really mean that the following are 'non-essential'. In putting forward these nominations, I invite us to think of how the Church of England can manage with less and yet do and be more, *locally*.

Diocesan communications and newspapers are non-essential. Dioceses just end up promoting the value of the centre to the parishes. Few parishes need a diocesan newspaper; even fewer read them. They are not, in any case, newspapers in the conventional sense. You'll never read a critical leader article about the bishop. This is *Pravda* world: a monthly PR communication to the outlets. In contrast, parish magazines are invaluable local resources and highly collectable, as they tend to tell you what is really happening – locally.

Equally, it is hard to find a diocesan communications team that reaches beyond its own constituents and makes any real public impact. There are sometimes reactive responses to be made in the event of occasional crises, but it is hard to see the point of proactive communications when the market for these is almost entirely for internal consumption.

Diocesan Mission and Evangelism presupposes that the diocese has a meaningful identity and value in the parishes and beyond. Bishops (in role) do, but few people in the Church of England have a commitment to or affection for their diocese. As an institution, the diocesan HQ is not likely to (ever) be a port of call for a baptism or bereavement visit. The Church of England is most alive and authentic in the local. And that is where its mission and evangelism is best understood. A post for Diocesan Mission established at the cathedral makes sense as the mother church of the diocese. Otherwise, there seems to be little value in creating costly central services that then have to be sold to the very people who have already paid for them.

Here I stick my neck out a bit – almost everything else that is left in most current diocesan HQs will also be non-essential. Stewardship? That exists in part to support central services and homogenize the giving across the diocese. It might be more effective to incentivize parishes differently, so that the funds churches raise locally were spent locally, or shared in local or missional projects, including overseas. Safeguarding? A considerable number of mainline denominations in the developed world don't recognize the concept or understand what the Church of England thinks it is doing. Danish Lutherans use the term *beskyttelse*, meaning protection, precaution, cover, refuge, shelter or shield. That is the conventional meaning of safeguarding. A recent conversation with a senior Danish Lutheran cleric was instructive, as they were utterly bewildered by the practice of the Church of England. As the cleric reasoned, if you have cause for concern about inappropriate behaviour, have a word with that person. If it is serious cause for concern, you could involve HR and introduce appropriate monitoring. If it is criminal cause for concern, use the police, courts and the criminal justice system.

It would surprise the Church of England if the local level of subsidiarity could divest itself of the frenetic organizational activism that is created by most dioceses and then demands more money off the parishes in order to feed the HQ's growing sense of self-importance. Diocesan HQs – and their growing numbers of 'chief executives' – have become soft instruments of bullying powers, pushing appraisals, demands, organizational language, mission targets, money targets, pressure to conform to uniformity and branding, and sign up to mission plans, vision statements, new strategies and more visions. If we are not careful, we are going to end up with a business infrastructure where we have one company HQ situated on some forgettable industrial estate, employing several dozen people but with no staffed outlets in the villages, suburbs and cities.

As the grip of our 'emergent ecclesiocracy' (a phrase coined by Jonathan Kimber) has increased in the post-war era, so our grasp of ecclesiology and public theology has weakened (Kimber, 'Ecclesiology and Leadership in the Church of England Today', 2014). Indeed, we may be running serious risks in talking up the prospects for growth and management, while on the ground the situation is escalating complex patterns of churchgoing, increasingly stretched resources, fewer stipendiary ministers, and ever greater pressures on clergy and churches. This is potentially quite serious for our national mission.

As Professor Linda Woodhead's research showed, the vast majority of the population remain well disposed to the Church of England (Heelas and Woodhead, *The Spiritual Revolution*, 2005). What puts them off, however, is too much talk from inside the church of money, management and numerical growth. The church – in continuing to stress these concerns – may imagine it is being proactive. But these foci represent reactive responses to wider cultural concerns, which can occlude the deeper character of the church. Our absorption with management, leadership, reimagining, vision, strategy and growth dominates our selection processes – from top to bottom. Correspondingly, it is rare to see an advertisement at the back of a church newspaper seeking a vicar who will lead a church into deeper theological learning or open up the riches of contemplative prayer to the wider parish. Let us hope and pray for a flourishing of the local church and chaplaincies, remembering that most of Christ's life and ministry was very localized and highly intensive. Only because of that did Christianity ever become extensive. We need a new revolution in the Church of England. *Maranatha*: come, Lord Jesus, come.

13

Post-Structural Values

In the Church of England, what is there to hope for at the moment? In chapter 12 we touched on diocesan newspapers – effectively regional 'trade journals' that market the diocese to itself. They cannot substitute for the absence of bishops, and it is hard to convey on paper or online warmth, empathy, care and compassion. The newspapers cannot replace the presence and engagement that local clergy and parishes need, any more than a parish magazine might substitute for the presence and availability of local clergy.

We have also explored the plethora – explosion, really – of 'central ministries' running out of diocesan HQs up and down the land, dealing with anything from discipleship to evangelism, mission to enabling, stewardship to lay education, well-being, youth work, pastoral care, and more besides. Sometimes the simplest questions are the best. Will anyone actually care or notice that the diocese has issued a statement on global warming? No. Might they pay attention if the bishop says or writes something on the subject? Perhaps. But it very much depends on whether the bishop has said anything new and worthwhile, or possibly controversial. Otherwise, it is unremarkable. Who needs to know that the bishop is currently concerned about the environment and other eco-challenges? Few, if any.

The emergence of diocesan central HQs has spawned a self-important and self-consuming culture that requires more and more money from hard-pressed parishes to feed a fantasy. That fantasy consists of the fallacious belief that if there is some kind of command-and-control bunker in each diocese, the messages, outputs and identity of the diocese can be controlled and promoted. However, few parishes pay much attention to what their diocese says, does or even means. It is, after all, a mere unit of governance and nothing more. It has no more right to affection, loyalty and respect than people might offer to North Humberside County Council or South Dorset District Council. So ask yourself this. After paying rates (taxes), and otherwise expecting the council to maintain the roads, pavements, schools and other services, would you be able to name who the chief executive of the council was, or any of the senior staff? Would their views on sexuality or slavery matter much, unless they were highly controversial? And in the light of this, why would a diocese expect to be more central in the lives of parishes and sector ministries? A diocese is, after all, just a unit of governance, in which the bishop exemplifies the office and role of a teacher and pastor to the people. We do not require another layer of governance or administration. Parishes do not need central organization and control.

In their recent book *Gen Z Explained*, Roberta Katz, Sarah Ogilvie, Jane Shaw and Linda Woodhead collaborate to explore the challenges that those born in and after the 1990s face, and also how they are coping with the world around them and tackling the tests and trials of the twenty-first century. The book is a riveting read and should be read by all bishops over the age of 40. Because what the book offers is respair: fresh hope. The book focuses on the distinctive ways of being, the values and world views shared by most Gen Zers.

What might you take from the book? Several things come to mind. First, values may be the new 'religion' of the twenty-first century. By values, I mean integrity, transparency, fairness, justice, truth, accountability, care, kindness and honesty. These are all forms of behaviour. Institutions and organizations that fail to exemplify these are not trusted by Gen Zers, and they will give them a wide berth. The Church of England fails all tests on this point alone. It will belong to the category of institutions to avoid, since (in the minds of Gen Zers) it only seeks your money, membership and loyalty. The failure to address sexism, homophobia, systemic opacity, the lack of clear and accountable governance – well, you do the maths. They won't join.

Second, the difference that Gen Zers will make in the world will depend on new forms of organization that cluster around the global challenges we face. These include our ecosystems, sustainability, accountability, equality, justice and freedom from oppression. The emerging protests of the Black Lives Matter movement give us textbook material for twenty-first-century socio-political organization and resistance. The movement does not depend on overt political or faith-based sponsorship, let alone patrimony or control. Churches and denominations can participate, but as equals, not as privileged stakeholders.

Third, the digital age gives Gen Zers access to communication and mobilization the like of which – in terms of revolution – we have not seen since the advent of printing presses and mass production of pamphlets and tracts gave birth to the Reformation in the sixteenth century. Revolutions come around quite often, at least one a century, and the serious, large-scale, tsunami-like ones every 300 years or so. Think the Black Death and the Peasants' Revolt. Think global climate change, famine and the ensuing French Revolution. Shortages of food, water and other basics mobilize populations.

The eco-catastrophes we are already experiencing lead to migrants and refugees. Gen Zers deal in causes, not just symptoms. More could be said here, but with these three challenges laid out above, it is clear that the Church of England is a long, long way off the pace. It does not read the signs of the times. It pines for a return to the Good Old Days – hence the Back to Church campaign – as though reminding people of what they might be missing is a 'good thing'. Gen Zers are well aware of what they are missing, and they will remain missing from the pews until the Church of England looks at itself in the mirror and welcomes the revolution it urgently needs.

But institutions tend not to organize their own revolutions. They will tinker at the edges with reviews and reappraisals. Sometimes, the only thing to hope for – respair – is the End Times, and a collapse. But do not despair just yet. Because decline and fall is inevitable, and what you have to imagine are the new forms that will emerge. They won't be fresh expressions, cell churches or church planting, or another injection of caffeine into the evangelistic bloodstream. Those are all old forms of faith that need to be quietly retired and allowed to pass away, as all things must pass. That said, history is sometimes kind and helpful to us. In this series of reflections we have been looking at an institution rusting and rotting from the inside out, and top to bottom. Yet within it, of course, the signs of hope were always there: the seeds of revolution and renewal, no less. Just as one example here, let us turn to sexuality, which even now causes enormous, heated exchanges and rowdy ructions in the Church of England and incoherent stances from our leaders.

Apparently, the Archbishop of Canterbury can censure Anglicans in the USA and Canada for their position on equal marriage but cannot censure Anglican bishops in Ghana, who voted for the recriminalization of homosexuality. He can intervene in one province but not in another. Gen Zers are not fooled by the hypocrisy and inconsistency this face shows to the world. They will give the Church of England a wide berth here. In Simon Goldhill's *A Very Queer Family Indeed: Sex, Religion and the Bensons in Victorian Britain* (2016), he explores the tolerance and forbearance of a bygone age. Edward White Benson was Archbishop of Canterbury from 1882 until his death in 1896. He was married to Mary (better known as Minnie) Sidgwick. To look at his CV, you'd think he was a pillar of the establishment. He went to university at Trinity College, Cambridge. He taught at Rugby and Wellington. From 1872 to 1877 he was Chancellor of Lincoln Cathedral. In 1874 he set up Lincoln Theological College. He was appointed as the very first Bishop of Truro, where he served from 1877 to 1882.

Yet Benson came from rather humble stock. His father was a manager at the British Alkali Works near Worcester. He went to grammar school. His roots were in the Midlands and in its industries. As a young man of 23, when he proposed to his 11-year-old cousin Minnie Sidgwick, Benson had been head of his family since his father's death a decade earlier. Minnie was also fatherless. Minnie's mother was unsure of the match, but they married seven years later when Minnie was 18. Minnie had no great attachment to Benson – or indeed to any other man. She 'batted for the other side' as the Victorians used to say, and her passions were always directed towards women.

With Minnie, Benson had six children, all of whom were openly gay. Nobody minded, least of all Gladstone or Queen Victoria, who saw this as no bar to the See of Canterbury. As Benson rose through the ranks of the Church of England, ending up as Archbishop of Canterbury, Minnie Benson's passions flowered into fulsome relationships, attracting neither abatement nor comment. As soon as Benson died in 1896, Minnie formed a very intimate relationship with Lucy Tait, the daughter of a previous Archbishop of Canterbury, and apparently lived with her until her death. One of Minnie's sons (Fred, the novelist E. F. Benson) wrote about his mother and Lucy sleeping together in his *Mapp and Lucia* novels. None of the Benson children ever married. Everyone seems to have known about this lesbian liaison, and many others. Nobody seems to have been bothered.

You could be forgiven for thinking this is all just an argument for Christianity passively accepting the cultural values of its age. But it isn't. Christians in every age have to weigh up what is to be accepted and what is to be rejected. All in the name of Christ, for truth, justice, humanity and hope. Earlier we mentioned the Danish Lutherans. Their stances in the twentieth century offer the Church of England an interesting and instructive model for being an authentic national church in the twenty-first century.

Danish Lutherans, like the Church of England, have the head of state (monarch) and Parliament to keep them in line. Yet the Danish Lutherans were able to take a lead from King Christian X in 1933, who became their first monarch to openly visit a synagogue. When war broke out and Denmark was all but occupied by Nazis, hardly any Danish Jews were deported to camps or perished. The stance of the monarch and the church was that all Danes were citizens. There is even an urban myth that King Christian X wore a yellow star throughout the war. Most Danish Jews were smuggled or evacuated to neutral Sweden. Danish Lutherans were among the first denominations to have female clergy. In 1948, the Minister of Ecclesiastical Affairs was asked by a parish if they could have a female priest. As Denmark already had full gender-based equality, the Minister ruled there was no legal obstacle.

A 2011 poll of the Danish public found that 75.8 per cent of the population approved of same-sex marriages being performed by the church. The figures for the population of England are now remarkably similar. In Denmark (pause, deep breath), the change duly happened, and by 12 June 2012 the Minister for Equality and the Minister of Ecclesiastical Affairs had introduced a bill approving same-sex marriage, which was passed in Parliament. Parliament also approved the wedding ritual with liturgy. The first same-sex couple was married on 15 June (not long to wait after 12 June!). Danes had long been used to same-sex unions being blessed in church since 1989.

It perhaps goes without saying that gay and lesbian clergy exist in Denmark (hardly breaking news), but their sexuality is regarded as a purely personal issue, and not the business of the bishop or others. Parish Councils in Denmark are central in selecting and employing new priests, including interviews with candidates. Note, these are Parish Councils, not PCCs. This means that the local population – not just folk drawn from the congregation – have a hand in choosing their minister, because the new minister will be for everyone, not just the faithful or actual church members. Conceivably, a local rabbi or mullah could be part of the interview panel. Indeed, why ever not? Once employed, parish priests are public servants and must serve all their parishioners, irrespective of faith (or none). Clergy cannot be discharged except for neglect of duties. So no parish priest is kicked out for being married, gay, lesbian or otherwise. This does seem pretty sensible and certainly civilized. Indeed, something like a proper national church, serving all the people. Locally.

So, we have reached the end of our reflections on rickety religion. Knowing that our national church is pretty rickety is an epiphany of self-awareness that the Church of England has yet to arrive at. It may be – probably will be – that the post-pandemic era causes the revolution that the church needs in order to be reformed and fit once again for national service. In the meantime, hang on to your despair. There is a long way to go yet, but, as Emma Percy's fine poem 'The Oil of Gladness' (2021) has it, we still have hope, and we are not alone. The holy balm of Jesus' birth, life, death and resurrection remind us all that our service to the world and worship are a nativity for all. We give thanks for that, and as the poem says:

> When setting out on a journey
> I pack a phial of precious ointment.
> This is the oil of gladness,
> a gift given me by the good angels at my baptism.
> It is distilled from the love of God for frail humanity.
> Perfumed with the sound of the dawn chorus, babbling brooks
> and the giggles of contented children.
> It has miraculous powers.
>
> When the way is uneven and unclear
> when the water is choppy or tempestuous
> when my body is weary and aching
> when my mind is fearful and depressed
> a few drops can lift my spirit,
> soothe my soul and restore my strength.
>
> Like all Holy gifts
> it is not diminished by usage.
> It is remarkable.
> There is no use-by date.
> The perfume does not fade nor the oil decay.
> It is in fact replenished through being shared.
> In worldly terms it costs little
> and can be had for the asking.
> So, I urge you to get yourself some.
> All you need is an open heart and a capacity for joy.

Reflections for Part 4

> Blessed are the gentle, for they shall inherit the earth.
> Blessed are those who mourn, for they shall be comforted.
> (Matthew 5.4–5)

Neil Douglas-Klotz's work has done much to help us grasp the nuances of Jesus' ordinary and everyday speech. We know that Jesus knew Hebrew, had some familiarity with Greek, and may well have been able to converse in other tongues when in Samaria, Gerasene or other Gentile areas. Knowing what Jesus might have actually said, rather than what the Greek, Latin or English translates as his words, is fraught with tricky speculation. Yet the real gospel message is usually far more subtle than we can know. This at least invites us to ponder the Aramaic that Jesus spoke and listened to. To know this is also to acclimatize ourselves to the world that Jesus inhabited.

We easily forget that our world is sensate. A visitor to Palestine-Israel today experiences a land full of aromas, sights, tastes and sounds. The scent of almonds, apples, sycamores, blossom, the odour of the Sea of Galilee, thousands of water-birds – egrets, herons and cranes – and the smell of fish, all nestle among the smells of humanity in towns, villages and cities. The black basalt hills above the Sea of Galilee, and the distinctive smell of the Dead Sea, with its thick, hot-dry air expelling even a hint of humidity, also pongs with an odour that can repel.

Yet the Galilee that Jesus inhabited in the first century – with its own aromas, sights, tastes and sounds – would have been rather different from that of the twenty-first century. It was much wetter, and the seasons more evident than they are now.

REFLECTIONS FOR PART 4

Pre-climate-change Palestine was naturally green and luscious. The parts of Palestine that Jesus would have known would have almost certainly included water buffalo and lions (they are in the Old Testament, and we have no reason to suppose that such animals were extinct in Jesus' day). The wild landscape in places could have comprised some dense, even tropical jungle. It would have been dark and a place of danger – but also where one could find edible food easily to hand. Land that was not farmed or used for pasture would have been abundant. There was desert and wilderness too.

The Aramaic word that Jesus uses, *taba*, is usually translated as 'good', and the gospel gives us lots of instances where Jesus uses this word. But what is 'good' for Jesus are things in their time: the coming of age, the ripeness, the readiness of God's kingdom, preparing for the way of the Lord, announcing the year of the Lord's favour at the synagogue. These are *taba* moments: moments when ripeness and maturity comes.

In contrast, the Aramaic word *bisha*, which is often translated as 'evil' in the Greek and then in English, is a term that means things that are out of their time (or season), or have been delayed in their progress or stunted in their growth or ripeness; or they may have become overripe and so become rotten, perhaps even self-fermenting.

In some respects, one cannot understand the parable of the wine skins and the wine until you know your *taba* from your *bisha*. Ripe things are for ripe skins. In the New Testament, the word *agathos* is often used for 'good'. For 'evil', the word used is *poneros*. But these words signal rather different cultural and linguistic ideas. The Greek idea of good versus evil focuses on human-to-human relationships, while the Aramaic terminology rests on the rhythm and timing of nature as an expression of unity and maturity.

So what Jesus is saying in the Beatitudes is tuning us into the very breath of God. We mature in Christ as we learn to be occupied by the breath and being of Jesus – filled gradually with the Holy Spirit. Our maturing is the result of incarnational ripening.

When one begins to imagine Jesus' Beatitude biddings in Aramaic, a whole new world opens up. Should we really love those who hate us, and pray for those who persecute us? This word 'pray' in Aramaic has the sense of inclining or bending towards or listening to. But what do you do with people who despise you? The Aramaic says you lean towards them and listen to them; you incline yourself towards them. And as you do, the snare is the open space for those who want to harm you but will perhaps capture them. Put another way, love is an open space and a bit of a honey trap. By inclining towards somebody and giving them the space, you create the ground or possibility for them to reimagine something quite different. We find this in John 13.34–35: 'I give you a new commandment: that you love one another ... just as I have loved you. By this everyone will know that you are my disciples.'

When we start to reimagine the Beatitudes in this way, we find ourselves challenged afresh in our faith. For example, I have taken some verses from Matthew 7.15–20, and in order to show the Aramaic concepts in this passage I have removed the language of good and evil and replaced it with that of maturity and immaturity, ripe and unripe:

> Beware of false prophets which come to you in sheep's clothing. But inwardly, they are like ravenous wolves. You will know them by their fruits.
>
> Do people gather grapes of thorns, or figs of thistles? Even so, every ripe (or mature) tree brings forth ripe (mature) fruit. But every unripe (immature) tree brings forth unripe fruit (hard, immature, sour or lacking taste?). A ripe (mature) tree cannot produce unripe fruit, and neither can an unripe (immature) tree bring forth ripe (mature) fruit. Every tree that ultimately fails to produce ripe (mature) fruit is cut down and is cast into the fire. By your fruits, you shall know them.

It does not matter whether we have fig leaves or sheep's clothing to camouflage wolverine tendencies. As Jesus noted on a number of occasions, 'By their fruits you shall know them.'

Our ripeness and maturity matters. Again, as with the salt of the earth earlier, the tree that bears no fruit has a use: it can give warmth and light in a fire. But the key to the Beatitude is waiting for the right kind of growth, maturity and ripeness. It is by our ripeness and maturity that we will be known.

Jesus was born into a world that knew the cycles, the seasons, the soils of his time. Ripening and things not being able to ripen would have had immediate resonance with his audiences. In some respects, therefore, our lives are the soil on which Jesus depends for seeds and fruits. One of the key lessons from the first few chapters of Genesis is that if you take ripeness for granted (take what is not yours, before you or it are ready), it is hard to cover up the glaring folly of this with excuses. Actually, no clothing can cover up presumption and hubris. Emma Percy's poem 'Fig Leaves' captures this:

> To have one's eyes opened
> To be confronted with the inconvenient truth
> And to see the consequences
> Of the comforting assumptions
> Leaves us uncomfortable
> Exposed, vulnerable
> And ashamed of our nakedness.
>
> No wonder time and again
> We practise the absurdity
> Of sewing fig leaves into loin cloths
> To cover our shame
> And, if we have the power,
> Conscripting acolytes
> To praise the glory
> Of our invisible clothes.

Ultimately, the Beatitudes are incarnational. They are incarnated and grounded. They are not like the Ten Commandments and virtues that we find listed elsewhere in the Scriptures. The Beatitudes are states of being and states of breathing: an invitation for God to prepare his home in our earthed bodies. Here I submit six new Beatitudes inspired by those of Pope Francis:

> Mature are those who stay true and constant when enduring all manner of evil and suffering, forgiving their persecutors and betrayers from the depths of their heart.
> Mature are those who see the discarded, diseased and demonised and marginalized and enfold them in their embrace.
> Mature are those who see God in every single human being and work to make us all also find Jesus in others.
> Mature are those who guard, cherish and tend our fragile earth and communities.
> Mature are those who relinquish their own sanctuary and security in order to reach out to others who lack health and safety.
> Mature are those who yearn, strive and pray and work for the unity that Jesus called the church and world to.

All of these can be the messengers of God's mercy and tenderness. Surely, they will receive from him their merited reward? Maturity and ripeness is what God does in God's time. It is making goodness out of the seed and the fruit, each in its own time. It cannot be hurried, and it will not be diminished.

Discussion

- What is your community bereft of, and mourning?
- What active comfort can your congregation bring to the community in its loss?
- What does your congregation and its ministry offer to those who ache in their grief – whether that is personal, social, cultural or economic?

PART 5

Churches and Cultural Climate-Change Denial

14

Learning from Canute

The myth of King Canute is one of those stories that you may remember from your childhood. Like one of *Aesop's Fables*, we may have lost the original point of the story long ago, but the tale nonetheless persists. Cnut the Great, also known as Canute (born 975 (?), died 12 November 1035), was King of England, Denmark and Norway, which were often referred to together as the North Sea Empire during his rule. As a Danish prince, Canute won the throne of England in 1016 in the wake of centuries of Norse invasion and settlement. Canute's later accession to the Danish throne in 1018 brought the crowns of England and Denmark together. Norway was added later, with a crowning at Trondheim. The earliest written record of the Canute myth comes from Henry of Huntingdon in his *Historia Anglorum* (early twelfth century). At the height of his ascendancy, Canute ordered his throne to be placed on the seashore as the tide was coming in. Then he spoke to the rising tide,

> You are subject to me, as the land on which I am sitting is mine, and no one has resisted my overlordship with impunity. I command you, therefore, not to rise on to my land, nor to presume to wet the clothing or limbs of your master.

But the sea came up as usual, and disrespectfully drenched the King's feet and shins. So, jumping back, the King cried:

> Let all the world know that the power of Kings is empty and worthless, and there is no King worthy of the name save Him by whose will heaven, earth and the sea obey eternal laws.

THE PRECARIOUS CHURCH

"He says there's no scientific basis for global warming."

© Clive Goddard, used by permission

This has become by far the best-known story about Canute, although in modern readings he is usually a wise man who knows from the outset that he cannot control the waves. Today's readers might look at this tale with fresh eyes in the light of climate change. Can we do anything to stop the rising, incoming tides? In a word, no. Despite wave power being harnessed, and extensive efforts in cutting carbon emissions that might slow the increasingly rapid melting of our glaciers and the warming of our oceans, things only seem to be getting hotter and wetter. As I write, we are gearing up to host the Global Climate Change Summit (COP26) in Glasgow. As gatherings go, I suspect we may look back on this moment in 50 years' time and wonder if we had done enough. Or could have done more. Or was it all just too little too late? The jury will be out on this for some time to come. None of this might seem to be immediately relevant to the churches. We seem to have our own worries, of which more later. True, denominations and church leaders do issue statements on climate change and ecology. These are typically messages of hand-wringing, spiced up with the usual care-for-creation virtue-signalling – but little on how that change accelerates poverty, deprivation and disease in the developing world. Some church leaders go further and announce ecclesial zero-carbon footprints, setting a date in the future by which time they will themselves have joined the choir invisible. There is also the odd gesture to nudge the faithful: the bishop driving a hybrid car, or the dean eating a burger entirely made of plant-based protein, or perhaps some solar panels to replace the church slate roof. However, the issue is much closer to home than you may think.

A senior colleague and friend hailing from one diocese in the east of England, and one that enjoys a lengthy coastline along the North Sea, was surprised to come back from a short sabbatical and be met by the recently appointed Leader of the Enabling Team, charged with delivering and rolling out the new Mission Action Plan for the diocese. Mission Action Plans are peculiar works. Imagine a recipe book written in a foreign language you are not familiar with, difficult to understand even with the illustrations, and for which hardly any of the ingredients are available in your local shops or have ever been heard of by local people.

If you can imagine that, then you will have some insight into the basic problem with Mission Action Plans. Yet such booklets are routinely churned out across our dioceses, and somehow must be read. Few will ever be remembered. These recipe books – for that is what they are – are not based on research, nor are they demand-led. None of the authors of Mission Action Plans normally bothers to ask 20 parishes and their clergy such questions as, 'How can we help?', 'What difference could we make to the stresses of ministry, and alleviate the strains faced by clergy and parishes?', and 'What would sustainability look like in your neck of the woods ... and what resources do you need just to keep going?' No, these are all the Wrong Questions.

The Right Questions are, 'How can we grow ... and also cut costs at the same time, and prune parishes and clergy we suspect are unproductive?' The writers of most missional recipe books are top-down folk by instinct, and hence their results in programme design. They know what the gospel is; what the church should be; what the people all need. There was no need to consult. They got all their know-how from the Bible, so there was no need to do any research or take the local pulse and ask some actual questions. This recipe-book approach does not emerge out of collecting local food stories and know-how. It is prick-and-ping microwave cooking; ready meals in minutes that just need to be reheated. But parishes don't need a strategy document for this; it is just air cover for enforcing compliance.

These piles of 'new', 'fresh' and 'inspirational' missional recipe books, mainly unread, grow ever larger. Producing these Mission Action Plans is committee work, but still top-down. Progress from the three-day meeting with the flip chart and Post-it notes to the final product – a glossy brochure replete with charts, maps, graphs, numbers, vision, testimonies, aspirations, quotes and photos of bishops doing something (usually with livestock), and pictures of young people smiling – had been expedited quicker than any super-fast fibre-optic broadband provider could manage.

Naturally, my friend and colleague had to be paid a visit by the Leader of the Enabling Team promoting the fizzy new Mission Action Plan, so everyone senior in the diocese was 'fully on board' with what it said. Compliance issues again noted. My friend and colleague studied the maps carefully, which showed where the new congregations were to be 'planted', and how the 'old parishes' were to be 'consolidated' into 'Missional Minster Areas'. The rural deaneries were to be replaced with 'active-out-facing resource hubs geared for equipping disciples and enabling transformation'. This would all be done and dusted by 2035. There was a new strapline too, as well as a prayer for this bold, adventurous endeavour (written by a committee) and lots of exciting projections.

Looked at on the map, and within the framework of this mission-planning exercise, this might have all made sense. But my friend, just back from sabbatical, asked if the authors had seen the BBC Weather app of late, and looked at the predicted 2035 climate change map for the UK, their region, and the diocese in question? It turned out this future map had formed no part of mission-planning groupthink. 'Well,' said my colleague, 'that map shows half the diocese under water, so most of these new congregations will be submerged. Worse still, our rural economy, tourism, fishing, shipping and port industries, and many of our current transport infrastructures will be decimated. Did the group think, at all, about *what kind of world* we might be living in by 2035? I mean, that is where our churches will be trying to exist, live and serve in a dozen years or so.' Answer back came there none.

15

Money, Sex and Power

One of the leading commentators on religion and politics in the USA is Robert P. Jones, who is the CEO of the Public Religion Research Institute (PRRI). His recent books on the churches and racism have rightly attracted high praise for their depth of research, the range of statistics he draws on, and the bodies he consults (Pew Foundation, several Washington DC-based polling and research centres, etc.). Best of all, perhaps, is his unimpeachable clarity, the boldness and frankness of his prescient analysis, and his conclusions and future projections. Few could easily argue with his devastating blend of data, history, cultural and political analysis, and his very nuanced feel for and understanding of religion in contemporary America. Granted, American Christianity has evolved differently from its European forebears. In the USA, the customer is king. Faith thrives on religious consumerism. It is also financed differently, with congregations, for the most part, paying their own way for their own plant, staffing and resourcing.

Even in classic 'mainline' denominations (Methodist, Presbyterian, Baptist, Episcopalian, etc.), individual congregations tend to set their own budgets, pay their clergy, hiring and firing at will. On a fact-finding trip some years ago now – looking at how diocesan infrastructure in a historic Episcopalian diocese operated – I was struck by the difference between expectations, and where the power in the Episcopal Church resided, compared to the British Anglican churches.

This US diocese was a well-run enterprise, but there were very, very few diocesan staff. Congregations (still called parishes, but not in the sense Europeans mean at all) that reached out to young people hired their own youth ministers. The bishop could not understand why you would need a Diocesan Youth Advisor, or why every Church of England diocese might. The conversation with the bishop produced the same shrug of the shoulders for paid officers for mission, evangelism, stewardship, ethnicity, disability, ethical investment and more besides. Congregations that had a vision for such ministry got on with it. They did not wait for their bishop or diocese to organize it for them. Those that did not offer a panoply of ministries – perhaps a small rural church dozens of miles from anywhere – were nonetheless working out something different, like how to care for immigrant crop-workers. Parishes raised their funds and, for the most part, kept the vast majority of what they raised for their local mission. The quota paid into central funds was miniscule – a notional 5–8 per cent, depending on need. Most of what the quota was collected for went to subsidize parishes that needed ministry support but could not afford it, and probably never would.

The number of diocesan employees that the bishop had at his disposal could be numbered on the fingers of two hands. The central resourcing from the diocese to the congregations comprised some legal advisors, some HR and mediation experts competent in resolving intra-congregational conflict, and some administration, including financial. The bishop did not think it was remotely strange that more than a third of his congregations had staffing levels greater than the diocese. Or that many of his own clergy were paid more than him. More recently, the diocese mothballed its cathedral for a range of reasons, including financial. As the bishop could not justify subsidising a cathedral that had become insolvent, the diverse ministries in that city are now shared between the neighbouring parishes. Meanwhile, the cathedral remains open, but only when the culture and demographics change will its role in ministry be rekindled.

While I am not suggesting for a moment that the American model translates to Europe, the refreshing pragmatism of the US Episcopalian dioceses is mirrored in other mainline denominations. Bishops are therefore left to function as the Ordinal requires: caring for the clergy, teaching through scholarship and study, speaking out on behalf of the voiceless, and only when necessary speaking for the diocese too. My US bishop colleague was bewildered by my description of the episcopal and diocesan portfolios and expectations in England. 'No one would fund that here ... or expect a diocese to provide those services,' he said.

The pragmatism of American Christianity is puzzling and perhaps perplexing for their older European cousins. Doing what works is different from doing what is right, and American Christianity – perhaps especially its Evangelical expressions – has produced some novel and heterodox forms of faith that are ethically and doctrinally questionable. However, for around a century, the combination of pragmatism, consumerism, post-war productivity and wealth, with increased social mobility, has come together to provide the richest of soils for an American Evangelical boon. Offshoots have emerged, too, that are Charismatic, neo-Pentecostal, and health, wealth and prosperity focused. Evangelicalism has also penetrated Hispanic and emerging Asian communities.

Robert P. Jones, however, notes the unseen and darker side of this success. He traces the roots of Evangelical growth and success in part to white supremacy – white, male, privileged, entitled, educated and in control of the apparatus of social, financial, economic and political power. (See his *The End of White Christian America*, (2016) and *White Too Long* (2020).) He sees this domination coming to an end, and with it the presumptuous hegemony of white Evangelicalism. He does not think this is at all bad. In other writings, Jones also suggests that the death knell for white Evangelicalism, while not caused by Donald Trump's rise to presidential power, was nonetheless reflected by his four-year sojourn at the White House.

We already know that 80 per cent of white Evangelicals voted for Trump. We know that this same constituency was far more drawn (note, more than other Christian groups) to conspiracy theories such as those perpetrated by QAnon. While some readers may find this hard to compute, one should recall that most of the major religious conspiracy theories (from the 1960s to the end of the twentieth century) on the identity of the individuals or corporate bodies in league with the Anti-Christ, Satanic forces and End Times calamity originated from white Evangelicalism. QAnon was just another supply of fresh manna for hungry white Evangelicals. A cabal of Satanic paedophiles operating a global child-sex-traffic ring and conspiring against former President Donald Trump in his term in office was never that hard for biblical literalists and fundamentalists to swallow whole.

Likewise, white Evangelicals are more likely than any other Christian group to: deny climate change and see it as a conspiracy; oppose equal marriage and more generally gay rights, including gay people serving in the military; work and pray for abortion to be re-criminalized and have considerable empathy for and lend support to protesters barracking outside medical clinics providing this service; not be too concerned by Confederate flags; be anti-immigration, and in favour of harder borders and expulsion; be Islamophobic, including believing that Barack Obama is a Muslim; and be less likely to sympathize with Black Lives Matter and be more inclined to take the side of law enforcement (that is, police) in the event of violence against persons of colour.

English Anglican Evangelicals may feel a little queasy at these findings. After all, is this not the same constituency that spawned thousands of evangelism courses and megachurches? And growth is good, right? I mean, isn't that the point of the church ... to grow and keep growing?

16

Forecasting and Futurescapes

If English Anglican white Evangelicals thought the analysis of Robert P. Jones represented a range of subjects on which they'd rather not comment ('... Let's just get back to those Mission Action Plans, church-plant, grow, grow, grow ...' etc.), then he has done some more calculations and projections for us to wrestle with. As he is charting the deep and rapid changes in the cultural currents, his data and research should give yet more cause for concern to white Evangelicals in the UK and USA. We have known for some while that Evangelicalism still seems to be the best at attracting young people to church. Evangelicals have certainly assumed this. They usually go one step further here, making the apparently logical deduction that more young people must mean the future of the church also belongs to Evangelicals.

But appearances can be deceptive, and this hubris has been checked in the first quarter of this century by the rapid fluxes of culture change among Evangelical youth. They are not necessarily against equal marriage, are likely to have gay and lesbian friends, and likely to have friends who are Muslim, Hindu or Buddhist. While Evangelicalism remains committed to evangelism, this emerging generation is probably more committed to tolerance, diversity, equality and inclusion.

Young people are different. They value sensitivity, mutual respect of differences, and otherness. They are against discrimination on grounds of gender, sexuality, disability and ethnicity. They are likely to be advocates of equality for minorities. This means that targeting, grooming and coercing their peers – this used to be called evangelism in universities – has become a mode of Evangelicalism that many millennials and Gen Zers now want to keep a safe distance from. The emerging generation of Evangelicals no longer read books from 'approved' publishers that strain and stretch to offer highly tenuous scriptural ground rules for sexual relationships. Nor do they join prayer meetings for supporting missionaries in predominantly Muslim countries. In short, most of these emerging Evangelicals are quite different from anything that has gone before them.

That is a huge cultural climate change, and most Evangelicals I know over the age of 50 are just in denial about it. They are working with old weather maps and forecasts, and they dwell in spiritually insulated, double-glazed, centrally heated bubbles. Many of our Anglican Evangelical bishops fall into this category. True, they were never pro-Trump. But they are into cultural climate-change denial in a big way. They still believe in old-style missions, and their gospel-speak and faith language increasingly sounds hollow and inauthentic in an age that values integrity, humility, forms of social and civic service, and kindness.

But Robert P. Jones has more surprises in his data and findings. For the first time in a century, mainline American denominations are performing *better* than their Evangelical rivals. That is, not catching up. They are ahead in the polls. Now, in truth, all parts of the church are in decline; sexuality, sexual-abuse scandals, the churches putting reputation and survival before authenticity, truth and integrity are just some of the reasons why emerging generations are not joining churches at all. Young people remain spiritual but are not religious. However, the churches that do champion the poor, foodbanks, social justice, climate change, refugees, asylum seekers, equal marriage, equality for women, and more besides, are now ahead of Evangelicalism in polling for attendance for the first time in almost a century.

Some may rejoice at this news. A few may think the trajectory of the inter-ecclesial Cold War (e.g., the Christian Union versus the Student Christian Movement) has seen a reversal. But this is not what it seems. For, as Jones points out, cultural climate change is challenging all denominations. The white Evangelical voters that put Trump in the White House may now be in steep decline. But it does not follow that the children of those voters will switch to mainline denominations in large numbers. True, some have, and are no doubt attracted by the progressive values and politics these churches exemplify. But the rising seas of cultural change are ones that affect all churches, and the signs are not encouraging. To paraphrase Canute:

> Let all the world know that the power of bishops is empty and worthless, and there is no church leader worthy of the name save Him by whose will heaven, earth and the sea obey eternal laws.

Where does it end? What does the futurescape look like? J. G. Ballard wrote a fine science fiction novel published in 1962, entitled *The Drowned World*. Ballard imagined a dystopian London of the future that had mostly disappeared, submerged by flooding and rising seas. The inability of humanity to control the climate – and our failure to understand how, by positive actions and self-limitation, disaster and dystopia could be averted – shape the context for the novel. In some respects, the churches face the same issues culturally. There is little that churches can do to change the environment around them. They can take some positive action, and also exercise self-denial, enabling the common good.

By self-denial here, I do not mean some narrow Lenten discipline. Rather, self-denial is a moral and spiritual discipline, which may mean, for example, that no matter what churches and church leaders think about equal marriage, they accept the cultural change and adopt it with grace as an act of public service. Philip Jenkins' recent *Climate, Catastrophe and Faith: How Changes in Climate Drive Religious Upheaval* (2021) shows how the shocks of sudden climate change in the past produced famine, social upheaval, violence and mass migration. In turn, these changes were interpreted in the religious beliefs and practices of their times: apocalyptic visions, revivals, new religious movements born (and then persecuted), religious violence, scapegoating, persecutions, witch-hunts (literally), victimization, internecine conflict between denominations, and end-time prophecy. We are entering that age again.

The evidence has been with us for some while, but our church leaders have shown little self-awareness in reading the signs of the times, and how cultural climate change has slowly overwhelmed the churches. The symptoms have predictably manifested themselves in the more secondary issues of money, sex and power. In fact, we should be watching out for the Four Horsemen of the Apocalypse: famine, plague, war and death. Our church leaders are not paying attention to this rising sea-change. The 'dearth' (as Philip Jenkins dubs it), is the lack of food, water and future that is already upon us, and is now leading to the largest movement of mass migration our world has ever seen.

This dearth arises from the very death of the earth, and the migrants travel, seeking new life and hope. It is to these global issues that churches should turn. Not with bland sentiments, but with serious action that slows and stables each of the Four Horsemen. How can we help those facing famine, plague, war and death? This is now the frontline of our mission and vocation in the twenty-first century. To be sure, money, sex and power remain fissiparous and divisive matters for churches at the best of times.

But perhaps what churches have failed to grasp in the last 25 years is that, however our internal wrangling has been conducted, social media and 24/7 news coverage means that the world can tune in and watch anytime, and without drawing near or joining a congregation or denomination. On the whole, the world has not liked what it has seen and heard.

In the court of public opinion, churches are regularly weighed and frequently found wanting. We don't do transparency and accountability. We don't do fairness. We preach about justice but won't sign up to the Human Rights Act (1997). Observers notice this. No Mission Action Plan, Strategy, Governance

Review or Bold Rebrand can address the deep cultural chasms that have opened up – and continue to multiply – between normal standards and shared values in public life, and how the churches actually act. Reputation management and PR from the churches cannot bridge this gap either. The sea is washing over the very legs of the churches, yet our church leaders still seem to think they can turn back the tide. They can't.

It would be much better if we shifted to more solid and higher moral ground. Or, if we can't change our ground, and to borrow a slogan from Donald Trump, is it time to drain the swamp? Otherwise we will continue to be bogged down. Draining the swamp would mean becoming congregations and denominations that were unequivocally in favour of equality, transparency, fairness, justice, truthfulness, integrity, humility and accountability. It would mean an end to trying to find some middle way between sexism and equality, or to 'affirming' people in same-sex relationships or equal marriage yet not actually treating them equally. We keep putting the reputation of the church before accountability and transparency. The churches will not be saved by PR agents or some new 'comms strategy'. Only the mercy and grace of God can save us now.

We need leaders who understand this, and who begin with their own repentance, humility and humanity. Everyone sees through what the churches are trying to do to evade scrutiny and accountability. The public can see it for what it is. Churches are only pretending to themselves. We currently have far too many church leaders in cultural climate-change denial mode. They fool no one but themselves.

Yet the cost of their ongoing denial continues to fall on us all. Sometimes the only way to effect change and avert disaster is to reject and eject the very leadership that holds us to ransom in this headlock and then pegs us back. Their vested power interests are no longer in the interests of serving wider society, or even right for the church. We may now need some cultural climate-change activists in our churches, taking direct action to end systemic abuses of power and privilege.

We are entering an era in which the only way to reform the

church is to protest and resist, even daring to withdraw, just as the first Protestants did. Our scriptures and faith emerged out of lands and cultures that were at the constant mercy of climate change, bad harvests, locusts, plagues, disease and wars. We can barely imagine that world, in which the very survival of any community or race depended on kind seasons, peaceful living and collaborative labour. Our planet is now out of kilter, and we need church leaders, as never before, to practise fearless care and courageous prophetic activism in our service to the world.

As the prophet Jeremiah said: 'Harvest is over, summer is ended, and we have not been saved' (Jeremiah 8.20). But neither are we doomed. Yes, the time is short, the harvest perilous, and the labourers few (Matthew 9.37). We don't have much time to put things right. We will need to work together. That will require some serious levelling down of existing powers and authorities in the leadership of our churches. And laity, clergy and churches must be levelled up, so our local Christian communities become the Arks of Salvation they are called to be. Even as the rains fall, and the waters continue to rise around us, there is always hope.

Reflections for Part 5

Blessed are the peacemakers, for they shall be called children of God. Blessed are those who are persecuted in the cause of righteousness, for the kingdom of Heaven is theirs.
 Blessed are you when people abuse you and persecute you and speak all kinds of evil against you falsely on my account. Rejoice and be glad, for your reward will be great in heaven; this is how they persecuted the prophets before you.
(Matthew 5.9–12)

In Emma Percy's poem 'Blessed are the Peacemakers' we see something of how demanding this Beatitude vocation can be:

We all want to be peacemakers
reconcilers, bearers of hope.
Yet, we gloss over the cost.
Peace-making, peace planting
is hard work.
Heavy lifting is needed for ground clearance.
Diplomacy for de-cluttering.
There will be anger as you
remove false idols from pedestals
and violence as you name
injustice and dismantle walls.
For peace to flourish,
rights of way must be reclaimed,
level playing fields constructed,
fortified borders breached,

barricades torn down,
swords turned into ploughshares,
privileges laid aside
and differences embraced.
To do this work,
to commit to this labour,
requires a pure heart
and a confident faith.
Blessed are the peacemakers
For they are the children of God.

The kingdom that God has sought to establish transcends nations, tribes, races and classes. This kingdom is one of sublime equality in which the poor and the beggars are fed, the lame can walk, the blind see. It is a kingdom that values service above leadership. How can it be extended? It cannot be packaged like a party manifesto, nor can it be something equated with something that the church is. Nor is it a utopia.

The revolutionary state is one in which by losing ourselves we gain. Jesus often criticizes those whose actions do not match their words, more than he praises those who live by their beliefs. There's no need to praise them, as they are already thriving. It is the lost sheep who need the attention, not the saved ones. The story of the good Samaritan condemns two people, the priest and the Levite, and praises only one. Jesus ends that parable by saying: 'Now, go, and do likewise.' The injunction is nearly always the same: 'Do.'

In Frank Field's illuminating book, *The Politics of Paradise: A Christian approach to the Kingdom* (1987), Field explores what it means to be a Christian approaching politics. He contended that the answer lies in each one of us, in our individual and collective responses. Christianity is not a religion: it is a way of life, and it is a blueprint for living. The nature of politics is much more about our attitudes than a set of programmes. Only by understanding that Jesus' project, the kingdom of God, is an inherently political project, which is about the redistribution of power, about humility, gentleness and faithfulness, will we understand that the kingdom of God is not meant to be the church.

Jesus' most angry denunciation of hypocrisy comes in one of his long rants against scribes and Pharisees in Luke 11. It is full of invective for those who preach one thing and do another, who make the pretence of long prayer but lack true goodness and godliness. Jesus calls them 'blind guides, straining out a gnat, and swallowing a camel' (Matthew 23.24). Deeds not words might be one of Jesus' mottos; deeds not creeds might be even better.

This message has often been lost by the followers of Jesus. We often think it would be important to think or believe the right thing, but for Jesus and for God, believing the right thing is as nothing to doing the right thing. A despised Samaritan probably believes many wrong things, but does the right thing. The Levite and the priest believe the right thing but just don't have it in their hearts to do the right thing. The case for rejecting worldly concerns is better built on the idea of poverty as an unburdening.

When we read the Sermon on the Mount, we can see that this lengthy set piece Jesus delivers in the Gospels takes his followers to new places: 'Don't take any thought for your life: what you will eat or drink, or for your body or what you'll put on.' Two of the reasons for this indifference, which he gives and justifies, are that wealth and possessions clutter things up.

The first is a familiar and uncontroversial idea that there's more to life than material things, but the second is perhaps a bit more startling: wealth is pointless. Jesus also goes on to say that earthly goods are corruptible, but the goodness, what we leave behind by our deeds in this world, will outlive us. In the same way, the Sermon on the Mount teaches us that being persecuted for righteousness is something that is a blessing.

These 'New Beatitudes' by Anna Blaedel[1] are drawing very near to the heart-core of what Jesus' words would have felt like and been received as when he first spoke his words. They speak to our condition, just as Jesus' words would have chimed with his listeners as he sat down to teach:

REFLECTIONS FOR PART 5

blessed are you who are raging.
blessed are you who are mourning.
blessed are you who feel numb.
blessed are you who feel sick. and tired. and sick and tired.
blessed are you who refuse to turn away.
blessed are you who need to turn away.
blessed are you who keep breathing deep.
blessed are you who are tending to your own needs.
blessed are you who are tending to the needs of another.
blessed are you who have been calling.
blessed are you who have been organizing.
blessed are you who have been testifying.
blessed are you who have been hearing.
blessed are you who have been resisting.
blessed are you who feel broken open beyond repair.
blessed are you who are raw beyond words.
blessed are you who are working hotlines and crisis care centres and bearing witness to the forces of violence and trauma unleashed and unloosed.
blessed are you who are marching.
blessed are you who are weeping.
blessed are you who preach and know that divinity resides in despised, abused, violated flesh.
blessed are you who know deep in your bones that you are good. and beautiful. and beloved. and sacred. and worthy. and believed. and held. and capable of healing beyond your wildest imagination.
blessed are you who remind others they are good. and beautiful. and beloved. and sacred. and worthy. and believed. and held. and capable of healing beyond their wildest imagination.
blessed are we when we dare to dream of a world without sexual violence, without white supremacy, without misogyny, without police brutality, without anti-trans and anti-queer violence.
blessed are we when we stay tender.
blessed are we when we stay fierce.

blessed are we when we dare to imagine repair, and transformation.
blessed are we when we labour together to make it so.

Ultimately, the fragility and injustices endemically present in the human condition, the challenges of our age, the demands of our time and the tumult of nations, society and our communities ask us to invest in maturity. This is what can hold us all to account, and also hold the broken. This is what can make the space for hope, which can ripen into life abundant. This is the groundwork enabling love to be shared and multiplied. This is the hallowing of God and of all made in God's image – faith that feeds us. In such a time, there is no space for denial, false hope or ideological fantasies. We need grounded leadership in church and society that does not just face the truth. It must also speak it, and make it real, so that justice and redemption can be established.

Discussion

- Describe the social and cultural climate of your community. Where are the micro-climates and discrete ecologies? What is the gospel for these people, places and spaces?
- We cannot do much to change the cultural climate and social weather, but nor can we deny it. What shelter do we offer to our communities for those who suffer from the challenges and ravages of change?
- How can we dialogue and debate with church leaders who are cultural climate-change deniers and want to continue as they always have?

Note

1 https://enfleshed.com/.

PART 6

Respair in a Time of Tumult

17

Respair in a Time of Tumult[1]

I have written about *respair* before. As a noun, *respair* means 'the return of hope after a period of despair'. As a verb, *respair* means 'to have hope again'. Although both forms are rare and obsolete, they seem ripe for reviving.

Most readers will be more familiar with the term *despair*, the verb, noun and experience. I despair of my football team. I despair of the government. 'I despair, therefore I still am, just about ... I think ...?' (with apologies to Descartes). Despair is, oddly, the place we end up in when there is nowhere else to go. The heart already broken into a million pieces cannot be broken into more. We are one step away from returning to our form as dust.

Yet despair is a place, and strange though this may sound, it is a temporary state and place for most of us, while we are gradually repaired. It is a time for some self-compassion, and that requires honesty and realism. The things that have brought us to this place may still be in place. But we cannot escape from despair by trying to make ourselves happy. The repair that can come out of despair must face the darkness that has surrounded us. Until we know this – and by that, I mean understanding and accepting – we will struggle. We will tell ourselves that if we can avoid despair there may be hope. On the contrary, the despair has to be unpacked and owned before it can be left.

In an age when feelings have been elevated to a level of existential status, we need to ask if we are still able to educate one another, or only able to score points off each other from the comfort of our swivel chairs.

The Church of England has retreated – ever so slowly – into its own echo chamber. It was once a support-based institution, but has collapsed into a members-only organization. Local clergy and chaplains heroically resist this trend, and do what they can to continue serving their constituencies and communities, despite the demand to focus on membership drives. Here, the leadership of the Church of England has been seduced by faddish managerialism and brand-strategizing.

With a sharp decline in affiliation (of any kind) to the Church of England, and a rising tide of cultural disenchantment with its leaders, a serious crisis is emerging. In recent decades, the Church of England has invested significant time, energy and money in branding, marketing, mission and reorganization. Every initiative has resulted in greater public distancing from the Church of England, and a steeper decline in attendance.

The Church of England leadership now functions like some unaccountable executive in a political party (communist, pre-Berlin wall) that cannot step outside its own bubble. Speeches at conferences get longer, the agenda less relevant, and the procedural motions riddled with minor points of minutiae. Party loyalists are rewarded and dissenters quickly distanced. Or, if they persist, denounced and denigrated. There is a whiff of dictatorship in the wind.

Culturally, we have reached a moment when even in the churches, dissent and disagreement are treated as disloyalty. The motto of the Anglican Communion is 'The Truth shall set you free'. That will therefore mean engaging with the reality of disagreement, not pretending it isn't there. It means honouring probing questions and dissenting opinion. It does not mean pushing a fiction that there is a 'common mind' when there isn't one. Frankly, as any couple or family will know, engaging honestly with difference is much more productive than pretended agreement. If so for our familial and intimate relationships, then surely so for the churches too, including the Anglican Communion? Asam Ahmad writes in the magazine *Briarpatch* (2 March 2015):

In the context of call-out culture, it is easy to forget that the individual we are calling out is a human being, and that different human beings in different social locations will be receptive to different strategies for learning and growing. For instance, most call-outs I have witnessed immediately render anyone who has committed a perceived wrong as an outsider to the community. One action becomes a reason to pass judgment on someone's entire being, as if there is no difference between a community member or friend and a random stranger walking down the street (who is of course also someone's friend). Call-out culture can end up mirroring what the prison industrial complex teaches us about crime and punishment: to banish and dispose of individuals rather than to engage with them as people with complicated stories and histories.

Asam Ahmad added to these reflections in a follow-up article for *Briarpatch* (29 August 2017). He notes:

> But sometimes the only way we can address harmful behaviours is by publicly naming them, in particular when there is a power imbalance between the people involved and speaking privately cannot rectify the situation.

He then concludes:

> It is important to note here that there is often a knee-jerk reaction to name many instances of conflict as abuse: the word 'abuse' can end up referencing a range of harm, from sexual and physical violence to gaslighting and even straightforward meanness.
>
> But at the same time, we must listen to survivors of sexual and/or physical violence, particularly when they tell us they have not been able to receive accountability through private interactions alone. Survivors publicly naming their abuser are often met with a refusal to listen to their stories, and with tone policing, gaslighting, and/or generally being dismissed.

This, despite the fact that survivors going public often do so at an incredible personal cost, and often after years of having tried to privately rectify the situation.

When we insist that all of these conversations must remain in the private sphere, we are insisting that accountability is always a private matter. The history of our movements very clearly shows the opposite is often the case. People continue to take the side of those with more power, more privilege, and more capacity, and often these people are never held accountable for the harm they have caused. This is precisely why call-outs [sometimes] need to happen.

Synod is in an occasional long-distance commuting relationship with reality. The public no longer support or trust a body that is not credible or relevant to their daily lives. Operating inside a culture of privilege and patrimony, and even unaccountable to loyal members, will not win new converts to the cause.

Aspects of the Church of England still constitute an important element of our collective national treasure. At local levels, parish ministry and chaplaincy continue to be cherished and valued, making appreciable differences to community and civic life. Yet that is translating less and less into church attendance. The more the central governance of the church tries to invent new initiatives to address its own numerical anxieties and other neuroses, the more the public back away.

Yet the leadership of the church lives in denial, and General Synod is an echo chamber for convincing the leadership that there is progress, when in fact the external evidence all points to disrepair and decline. If we were to conduct a cultural weather forecast for the future of the Church of England, the climate change will – Canute-like – swamp it within the next 50 years. Already drowning in irrelevance, it cannot resist rising cultural tide changes.

What is needed here is serious collective self-criticism. I doubt, however, that General Synod, the Archbishops or the Archbishops' Council can manage that. Fear of loss (face, support and control) means the grip only gets tighter, and the politics and practices meaner. Asam Ahmad, in *Briarpatch* (2 March 2015) notes:

> It isn't an exaggeration to say that there is a mild totalitarian undercurrent (even in) how progressive communities police and define the bounds of who's *in* and who's *out*. More often than not, this boundary is constructed through the use of appropriate language and terminology – a language and terminology that are forever shifting and almost impossible to keep up with. In such a context, it is impossible not to fail at least some of the time. And what happens when someone has mastered proficiency in languages of accountability and then learned to justify all of their actions by falling back on that language? How do we hold people to account who are experts at using anti-oppressive language to justify oppressive behaviour? We don't have a word to describe this kind of perverse exercise of power, despite the fact that it occurs on an almost daily basis in progressive circles.

Though we still lack a word for this, I could hardly put it better myself.

Re-mortgaging the church

It is hard to imagine the Church of England hanging on to its powers and privileges in the next 50 years. Especially since the majority of citizens expect equality and accountability from their institutions as any prerequisite for trust. Moreover, as the number of paid-up members of the Church of England has already effectively fallen of the cliff-edge – and there is no sign that this decline is temporary or seasonal – serious questions have to be asked. These relate to the fitness and role of an established church in one nation, yet within a devolved union of three nations and Northern Ireland.

The present state of the Church of England would pose an enormous challenge for the very best estate agent to elicit serious interest. True, the Church of England is not for sale. But it is constantly on the lookout for long-term and loyal tenants who will take care of the storefront as though they were the owners. Upkeep, appearance, productivity, regional-brand compliance and purpose are devolved to the local occupiers, who mostly do an extremely good job on very tight budgets.

For all their labour, laity and clergy will receive little thanks from their somewhat distant landlords, who are only interested in the productivity and turnover. And compliance too, unless diversification delivers growth. We now have a situation in which the Church of England's senior leadership are re-mortgaging the church on a regular basis. (Indeed, at the time of writing, the Church Commissioners have just announced a £500 million bond, which will have to be repaid in the coming decades. It is unclear what the borrowing is secured against if the Church of England continues to decline.)

In this, they are banking on the past and borrowing from the future to try and resolve the present issues. As many will know with their own homes, it is risky, and only makes sense if the value of your property goes up. But as the social, moral, spiritual and intellectual capital of the Church of England is all in negative equity, there may be a default at any point.

Re-mortgaging the Church of England is a risky business. Local branches may want to start asking some quite basic questions. Who really owns this business? Who does it serve, and for what purposes? Who are these people in regional and national headquarters, telling us how to run things locally and cutting our support while increasing their own?

As the term *zugwang* denotes (in chess), every move the church makes is wrong and only makes the position of the church worse. Yet the player at the board cannot sit there and do nothing, as that will forfeit the actual match. The famous psychologist Jonathan Haidt once said that to understand the governing narratives of our time, we needed to 'follow the sacredness ... find out what people believe to be sacred, and when [you find that, and the people gathered], there you find rampant irrationality'. Yet faced with difficult choices and competing convictions, most of our church leaders set aside law and wisdom in order to accommodate all ardent opinions and belief claims. They embrace what I call Rampant-Sacred-Irrationality, which defies reason and facts. Rampant-Sacred-Irrationality in the Church of England dictates that competing convictions must be 'balanced', and somehow everyone deserves something.

In a telling article by Bailey Lemon (*Medium Magazine*, 16 February 2020), she examines the inherent contradictions present in a culture that speaks about being progressive, when in fact it is aggressive, oppressive and repressive:

> They talk about listening, being humble, questioning one's preconceived notions about other people and hearing their lived experiences ... and yet ignore the lived experiences of those who don't speak or think properly in the view of university-educated social justice warriors, regardless of how much worse off they really are. That is not to say that we should accept bigotry in any form – far from it. But I would go as far as saying that the politically correct mafia on the left perpetuates a form of bigotry on its own because it alienates and 'otherizes' those who do not share their ways of thinking and speaking about the world.

Lemon is talking about the Radical Left, but her analysis comfortably translates to the current culture of the Church of England in many dioceses, and most certainly that of the Archbishops. Lemon continues:

> I'm tired of the cliques, the hierarchies, the policing of others, and the power imbalances that exist between people who claim to be friends and comrades. I am exhausted and saddened by the fact that any type of disagreement or difference of opinion in an activist circle will lead to a fight, which sometimes includes abandonment of certain people, deeming them 'unsafe' as well as public shaming and slander. It is disgusting that we claim to be building a new world, a new society, a better way of dealing with social problems –

but if a person makes a mistake, says and/or does something wrong, they are not even given a chance to explain their side of what happened because the process of conflict resolution is in itself driven by ideology rather than a willingness to understand facts. Actually, in today's activist circles one is lucky to be given any sort of due process at all, while everyone is put under social pressure to believe everything they are told regardless of what actually occurred in a given situation. This is not freedom. This is not social justice. There is nothing 'progressive' or 'radical' about it, unless you are referring to fascism.

Again, the resonances with the current Church of England culture hardly need spelling out. Yet a culture where there is no accountability, transparency or scrutiny of bishops creates a seedbed for inequality and injustice. Bishops seem content to let this continue, and none call it out.

Do they apologize for their mistakes in the here and now? No. But they will sincerely and sanctimoniously say sorry for sins committed centuries ago, but not by them. Do they acknowledge that the institution they want to see supported is broken, frail and far from perfect? No. They tell us instead that progress is being made, we are all on a journey, and that things are much better than they were ten years ago, or since they came into office. Do they provide convincing evidence for this? No. But you are still meant to trust them. Should you? Let us leave that question open.

Rampant-Sacred-Irrationality

Rampant-Sacred-Irrationality (RSI) is also the acronym for Repetitive Strain Injury. They have some similarities, the most obvious of which is that they are painful and exhausting. Rampant-Sacred-Irrationality is everywhere, or so it seems. It describes the current state of abortion debates. Both sides are vehemently pro-life. Gun control in the USA is another.

Both sides believe gun purchase and ownership should be controlled, but have very different ideas about who should have a gun, when, where and why.

In our own country, Brexit delivered in spades on Rampant-Sacred-Irrationality. Did our best interests as a nation lie in one version of freedom and identity (that was anti-EU) or the other version that was pro-EU. People who have family – or who had been friends for decades – have split irrevocably on the pivot of Rampant-Sacred-Irrationality. Like some ancient or modern civil war, we find kith, kin, neighbours and friends creating dividing lines that separate those who adhere to their sacred (that cannot be questioned or debated) and those that challenge it, who must be repelled at all costs.

Debates on gender, sexuality, transgender, ethnicity and religion also pivot on Rampant-Sacred-Irrationality. If my experience and identity is my right to own, and cannot be questioned, then it becomes sacred. To challenge it, or seek compromise, will be interpreted as a violation. Suddenly, and somehow, in contemporary culture we have reached a point where everyone has a sacred right to be entirely believed.

Many also think that the right to be believed includes the right to be right. That can be irrespective of the reasoning, facts and hard data. Our brains are fully part of our bodies, and when our thoughts are challenged or perhaps attacked, the mind responds in the same way that the body does to an assault. Our minds close down to protect us from the blows. The mind forms a steel-like cordon around our thoughts, and then thinks about how to respond by going on the attack. Much of this cognition is self-justifying, rather like the reasoning for a just war might run.

Thus, our inner voice might say, 'Well, he said that, and he would think that, wouldn't he …? Because he's against me on this matter, so that point was designed to upset me and torment me on that other front.' If your mind decides your thoughts and beliefs are being attacked, it is more likely you will close down than open up. Such attacks and assaults are more likely to harden resistance, close down debate and create a toxic culture of right versus wrong, true versus false, and leads us to go hunting for what is wrong and false about the other person.

The rational response to alien ideas is either to try and understand them or to admit we don't and shrug them off. But our minds defend us, and all too often alien ideas are treated as threats to our existential reality, in much the same way as our bodies might respond to any perceived threat. Here, we see that even a person simply with different views to us can be perceived as an antagonist. In part, this explains why we can feel so *aggressive* towards people we disagree with. Truth decay in leadership starts when those in authority start to talk about 'alternative facts', or simply dismiss science, hard evidence and solid data.

We are used to hearing our politicians try this, and it has steadily eroded our trust and confidence in them. We no longer believe what they say, even when they tell us they are right. The culture of spin, dissembling and briefing has eroded moral, social and political capital to a huge degree.

That our church leaders now do the same is not only sad and shocking but also distressing, because it will produce the same culture of mistrust. Yet we now encounter, consistently, bad lessons learned from politicians and PR gurus, put on the lips of what were presumably, once upon a time, good bishops and decent people who had a sense of truth and justice rather than brand loyalty. But nowadays, it is all about maintaining some fiction of perfectionism.

My friend and colleague Professor Nigel Biggar thinks quite differently about faith and politics. One of us would be characterized as more right-wing and conservative. The other, left-wing and liberal. Leaving aside that neither of us trust these labels or categories, it would not take much to flush out our differences. (Although far more unites us than would divide.)

But how are churches – and the Church of England, especially – to resolve persistent divisions within a culture soaked and saturated with its own Rampant-Sacred-Irrationality? There are lessons to be learned from the past. The American

Civil War (1861–65) pitched the southern Confederate states against the northern Union states. The practice of slavery in the United States was one of the key political issues of the nineteenth century, and a primary cause of the Civil War.

For Anglicans – Episcopalians in the USA – the division was painful. The economy of the southern states depended to a large extent on slavery. The northern economy did not. Episcopalians split down the middle on this, albeit only for the duration of the war. But the legacy continues to this day. Incidentally, all denominations split like this during the Civil War, and many in the American churches, including Quakers in the southern states, were more persuaded by the economic arguments for slavery than those for emancipation.

Many in the Church of England also supported the separatist Confederates. We perhaps forget too easily that even after slavery was abolished in Great Britain, many individuals and companies continued to invest in such labour overseas. Churches and mission societies did too. Slaves were economic units for investment and the means of production.

The Church of England is unable to come to terms with the current issues posed by Rampant-Sacred-Irrationality. The church enshrines the rights of those who oppose equality on gender and sexuality. The separatists are protected – including their own bishops – because it is held that their beliefs and right to self-determine their identity cannot be questioned. Rather like the Confederates ordaining their own bishop to care for the pastoral needs of slave owners, it is hard to challenge the tension between personal legitimacy and corporate agreement. At the end of the American Civil War, the Episcopalian Church was reunited, and meekly but fully accepted that Confederate bishop as an equal.

An uncritical accommodation of Rampant-Sacred-Irrationality culture risks undermining the rule of law. Smokers may well be distressed that cigarette consumption in public has effectively been outlawed. Yet the reintroduction of smoking zones in restaurants or pubs, or for that matter in cinemas or on public transport, is not fair to the rest of the population.

Neither is sexism or homophobia fair. Sometimes, decisions are made for the common good that must overrule individual or collective appeals to personal claims on rights. We all have to breathe the same air and share the same living space. But the Church of England still has a soft spot for affirming discrimination in a variety of forms, and it makes provisions for those who want to perpetrate these on grounds of tradition. But like smoking, we might discover that this results in the death of us all, not just the smokers.

Respair, not despair – what remains

In Kazuo Ishiguro's 1989 novel *The Remains of the Day*, we are introduced to Stevens, a butler who dedicated his life to the loyal service of Lord Darlington at his stately home near Oxford, England. Told in the first person, the novel is set in 1956, when Stevens takes a road trip to visit a former colleague. As he travels, he reminisces about events at Darlington Hall in the 1920s and 1930s.

We learn that Stevens was in love with Miss Kenton (the housekeeper) at Darlington Hall, Lord Darlington's estate. Stevens and Miss Kenton failed to admit their true feelings for each other. Their conversations as recollected by Stevens show a professional friendship, one that at times came close to blossoming into romance, but emotional reserve and professional resolve mean that was a line neither dared to cross. Stevens remained distant and never yielded, even when Miss Kenton tried to draw closer to him. As the book progresses, we also learn that Lord Darlington was a Nazi sympathizer.

When they finally meet again, many years later, Kenton has married and is expecting a grandchild. Stevens later muses over his lost opportunities with Kenton. But he also comes to review and regret his decades of selfless service to Lord Darlington, who, he reflects, may not have actually been worthy of his unquestioning fealty.

Ishiguro's novel offers us soft yet brutal exposure to the

world view of Stevens and those he serves. Stevens champions dignity, emotional restraint and the special qualities that make English butlers the best. 'Continentals' are dismissed for their emotional incontinence and Celts for their fiery tempers. The English, on the other hand, are reserved, restrained and appropriately reverential. In a kind of slow parody, Stevens' elderly father – also a former butler dedicated to a life of service – is dying upstairs. Messages are sent to his son that his father is dying, but the reply is telling: 'I'm afraid we're extremely busy now ... but we can talk again in the morning.'

As the death of his father is imminent, the strain begins to show on Stevens. But he carries on regardless. As Salman Rushdie remarked '[Stevens is] destroyed by the ideas upon which he had built his life' (*Guardian*, 17 August 2012). Much like F. Scott Fitzgerald's *The Great Gatsby*, we have a story that is also a critique of class, deference and emotional constipation. Stevens is a character who believes the best way to control the external chaos is by making dignity and emotional restraint internally sacrosanct. So much so that the irrational sacredness invested in by Stevens is believed to deliver him both safety and reward. It does neither. There is also a sense in which Ishiguro's novel is an exploration of the unwritten constitutions in work, society, families and other groups that are held to be sacrosanct. To question these codes is to trespass; to break the club rules is to sin; to mock the conventions is to violate the group and all it holds sacred.

'Respair' is an old word that one hardly ever uses these days. The opposite of 'despair', 'to respair' is to have fresh hope, and to move beyond the gloom of desolation and despondency and have faith in the future. Despair is to see no light at the end of the tunnel. Or, if you do happen to glimpse a twinkling light in the distance, it is the proverbial train hurtling towards you – so time to run and hide. Yet there is hope.

Hope may be one of the most important virtues humanity has. It believes in better, so does not despair of the present (though some exasperation is normal and perfectly permissible!). Hope can maintain relationships in rocky times. It raises our children and educates them. Hope does not give up. It wants the best for others. It is deeply rooted in God's grace and goodness. It is turned towards a greater light and the promise of our best for all individuals, communities and countries being realized. And their best for you. It yearns, as we all do, for justice, integrity, peace, truth and kindness to flourish.

The very first words that God utters in the scriptures (Genesis) link to some of the very last words (Revelation):

God said, 'Let there be light.' (Genesis 1.3)

[The Eternal City] has no need of sun or moon to give it light, for the glory of God is its light ... The nations will walk in its light ... [the city] gates will never be closed ... and there will be no night ... they will not need lamplight or sunlight, because the Lord God will be their light. (from Revelation 21 and 22)

It is into the darkness and the formless chaos that God first speaks – and light appears. Light is the first thing in these opening verses of the scriptures that God declares to be 'good'. In a world where much tragedy brings darkness, and where much sin lingers in the shadows, we need to be reminded that the light God speaks into existence is 'good'. It is that constant reminder, in our everyday lives, of the utter goodness, provision and love of God's creative work.

In a world where even now, and in so many places, darkness overwhelms households, communities, nations and lives, we yearn for the coming of light. Beyond the global challenges, our own lives also cry out for light – those places and circumstances in our lives where darkness has overshadowed us and light seems far, far way. An end to restrictions, impositions, isolation and marginalization. An end to loneliness and suffering. An end to abuse and the shame and pain it brings. An end to wars, to injustice, to suffering, to poverty, to hunger. An end to darkness.

John's Gospel starts with the eternal story of God breaking in with light to our world and our lives. John reminds us – with words that need to constantly ring from our hearts and our lips in faith and protest – that though our world is wounded God has spoken: 'Light shines in darkness, and darkness could not overpower it' (John 1.5)

That word 'overpower' is rendered differently in other translations of John's Prologue. Older versions have 'comprehend' or 'overwhelm'. The sense of the Greek, however, is that the darkness cannot 'grasp' the light. It just doesn't understand it. In modern idiom, it doesn't 'get it'. The darkness of evil, iniquity and wickedness cannot understand light.

Our politicians, and sometimes even church leaders, when they speak in half-truths, know they speak in half-lies. Misleading, covering up, refusing transparency and humane accountability, sweeping things under the carpet: these are all the works of darkness. But God lifts the lid and speaks the light into these dark places and the nooks and crannies that cringe from exposure. Because God is the source of all light and life, the darkness will not overpower us. John tells us that in the birth of Jesus, God has entered into creation afresh – *respair* – to bring light and life to all. As John puts it: 'The true light that gives light to everyone was coming into the world' (John 1.9).

As we look across God's creation, our task is to affirm with God all that is good. Wherever darkness threatens to overpower, whether in the lives of others or in our own lives, let us remember that God has spoken the very first words in creation: 'Let there be light ... and God saw it was good.' God's reign of light, love, grace, justice and mercy cannot be overcome by the darkness.

Finally

One of the best-known stories we have about St Francis of Assisi is his calling. He heard the voice of God saying, 'Come, restore my church.' Weathered, beaten and in a state of disrepair, few would take on such a calling. Yet Francis did, understanding that a new commitment, zeal and passion for the gospel was needed if Christ was to be offered to the world in the present and future. Across the world at present, there is a crying hunger for a church that can fulfil its mission to serve rather than be a body of self-service simply in order to survive and prosper.

I am continually struck by the visions that underlie new buildings or initiatives. What do the architects and builders hope to achieve? Too often in the church we build defensive trenches, bunkers and inward-facing conversations and structures that barely acknowledge the world around us. All institutions can get themselves into this space. What started as a place for the exchange of ideas becomes an echo chamber. Sometimes it takes poetry and prophecy to imagine the alternatives. As I was contemplating this problem, I found myself outside the Scottish Parliament building in Holyrood, Edinburgh. As a building, it has an important story to tell about openness, hospitality and visionary thinking. The Spanish architect Enric Miralles designed the building, but sadly died before its completion. From 1999 until the opening of the new building in 2004, the Scottish Parliament was housed in the Church of Scotland's General Assembly Hall on The Mound in Edinburgh. With its committee rooms and debating chamber, the Hall was an ideal place to host the fledgling Parliament before it acquired its own site.

In one sense, Miralles' visionary contribution and the hospitality of the Church of Scotland complement one another; they offer us a hopeful parable. Both enable new space and hope to come into being. Neither is integral to the future existence of the new creation, but both are vital in their roles as mother and midwife. This is about the creation of open space to foster good debates and the exchange of ideas to create a common purpose founded on the wisdom of the collective. Here, I think, Edwin Morgan's poem for the opening of the new Scottish Parliament speaks well to our time.

> Open the doors! Light of the day, shine in; light of the mind, shine out!

We have a building which is more than a building.
There is a commerce between inner and outer,
between brightness and shadow,
between the world and those who think about the world.
...
What do the people want of the place?
They want it to be filled with thinking persons
as open and adventurous as its architecture.
A nest of fearties is what they do not want.
A symposium of procrastinators is what they do not want.
A phalanx of forelock-tuggers is what they do not want.
...
Open the doors, and begin![2]

Christian fellowship should be liberating. It cannot mean just sitting down with people we agree with. It means sitting with those we don't agree with, and bearing with them; enduring, and staying in that space. Fellowship that is agreeable because we share the same class, background, outlooks, jokes and likes is not what the kingdom of God ushers in. What Jesus seeks from us is to befriend the friendless, and to engage with and love our enemies. The church is a new kind of being and living together, and one that models hope for the world.

In conclusion, therefore, and for our respair, I have – magpie-like – taken a prayer, some liturgy, a little scripture and inspiration from Jürgen Moltmann and Desmond Tutu, and offer this new Canticle (a 'mash') as a script to recite prayerfully and antiphonally:

The kingdom of God means:
Nobody has been left alone in despair.
Nobody has to conceal their identity,
Nobody has authority to dominate and dictate others.
   Nobody.
Nobody is isolated or marginalized.
Nobody is deserted in their hour of need.
Nobody is a problem, and anybody is no problem.

Nobody is beyond God's love, reach and embrace. Nobody.
Everybody is called to bear with others.
Everybody is called to peace.
Everybody is called to live in hope, and make hope real for others.
Everybody is called to love, as Christ loves us. Everybody.
Goodness is stronger than evil.
Love is stronger than hate.
Light is stronger than darkness.
Life is stronger than death. For everybody.
In faith, hope and love, let us keep our minds fixed on what is true.
On what is good, just, pure and kind.
On what commands respect, is commendable and worthy of praise.
For then we shall be followers of Jesus' way. His Way.

Notes

1 First published online with Surviving Church, and edited by Stephen Parsons.
2 Adapted from Edwin Morgan, 'Open the Door!', https://archive2021.parliament.scot/visitandlearn/Education/56969.aspx.

Reflections for Part 6

> You are the light of the world. A city built on a hilltop cannot be hidden. No one lights a lamp and puts it under a tub; rather, they put it on the lamp-stand where it shines for everyone in the house. In the same way, your light must shine for people, so that they may see your good works and give praise to your Father in heaven.
> (Matthew 5.14–16)

'Respair' is the triumph of hope. It refuses despair to have the final word. Hope, of all things, is what keeps humanity human. The word 'respair' may have been coined by Andrew of Wyntoun, a Scottish poet and chronicler who lived between *c.* 1350 and *c.* 1423. The Latin roots of the word come from 'again' and 'hope'. Wyntoun was a Canon of St Andrews and, from about 1393 to his retirement because of old age in 1421, he served as prior of St Serf's, Loch Leven (Kinross, Scotland). Anyone who knows anything about Scottish history in this period will wonder how those living in such times avoid despair. Wyntoun's answer to the isolation brought by wars, famines, disease, raids, persecution and oppression was 'respair'. You are never alone. God abides. God loves. God is with us. Emmanuel.

Though we may be socially distant from one another by plague, pandemic, media, politics, faith or family divisions, the Gospels tell us we are not apart from God or one another. We are bonded together in faith, hope and love. We are bonded together in an act of recollection and remembering, where we turn back to the Servant King, the One Who Reigns from the

Tree and who bids us not to be melancholy, or even nostalgic, but rather to *re-member* this world of Christ's, as God would put it back together. That is, knitted together in acts of charity, love, service and sacrifice. Christ, in you, is the touching place between our humanity and society and God's abundant grace and divinity.

Jesus loves us all enough to come close to us. So close, in fact, that he will wash away all the mess, dust and dirt with water, some cloths and a towel. He holds our feet. He holds you. You can't wash someone's feet at a distance; you have to touch them. Frankly, there is no social distance in this. And there is no social distance between anyone and Jesus. He has drawn near.

In this extraordinary and moving poem by John O'Donohue ('This is the Time to Be Slow', 2008), he offers a sense of the right kind of hopeful remembering, not for what once was but for what might and shall be if we dare to live in hope:

> This is the time to be slow,
> Lie low to the wall
> Until the bitter weather passes.
>   Try, as best you can, not to let
> The wire brush of doubt
> Scrape from your heart
> All sense of yourself
> And your hesitant light.
>   If you remain generous,
> Time will come good;
> And you will find your feet
> Again on fresh pastures of promise,
> Where the air will be kind
> And blushed with beginning

The 'The Gate of the Year' is the popular name given to a poem penned by Minnie Louise Haskins. The title given to it by the author was 'God Knows'. She studied and then taught at the London School of Economics in the first half of the twentieth century. The poem was published in 1908 as part of a collection titled *The Desert*. It caught the public attention and popular imagination when the then Princess Elizabeth gave a copy to her father, King George VI – he quoted it in a 1939 broadcast to the British Empire.

The poem was widely acclaimed as inspirational, reaching its first mass audience in the early days of World War Two. Its words remained a source of comfort to the Queen for the rest of her life, and she had its words engraved on stone plaques and fixed to the gates of the King George VI Memorial Chapel at Windsor Castle, where the King was interred. You may know these lines:

> And I said to the man who stood at the gate of the year:
> 'Give me a light that I may tread safely into the unknown.'
> And he replied:
> 'Go out into the darkness and put your hand into the Hand of God.
> That shall be to you better than light and safer than a known way.'
> So I went forth, and finding the Hand of God, trod gladly into the night.
> And He led me towards the hills and the breaking of day in the lone East.

It is reassuring to know that, in these times, the touching light and hand of God is with us. The Gospel of John suggests that one of the key words or ideas to help us understand the ministry of Jesus is that of 'abiding'. The word is linked to another English word, 'abode'. God abides with us. Christ bids us to abide in him, and he will abide in us. He bids us to make our home with him, as he has made his home with us. And central to the notion of an abode is the concept of abiding.

To abide means to 'wait patiently with'. God has abided with us. He came to us in ordinary life, and he has sat with us, eaten with us, walked with us and lived among us. And died like us. In fact, died desolate and alone. (All but a few kept their social distance from Jesus at the cross.) Perhaps that is why John ends his Gospel with Jesus doing ordinary, close, social-sharing activities: breaking bread with strangers; walking on a dusty road with two puzzled disciples, grieving; eating breakfast on the seashore. God continues to dwell with us. He was with us in the beginning, and he is with us at the end. He will not leave us.

God is Emmanuel. He made us for company with each other and for eternal company with him. God is with us in creation, in redemption and, finally, in heaven. God with us is how John's Prologue begins – the Word was with God; he was with us in the beginning. God is with us in the valley of the shadow of death; he is with us in light and dark, chaos and order, pain and passion. And though we may turn aside from him, he will not turn from us. And in the resurrection, Jesus is again with us – more powerfully and intensely than ever.

God is with us. God is with us where we are, right now. When you think you are just about hanging on. But only just. And just when all seems dark and hopeless. There is a light.

Discussion

Light is essential for all life that lives above the ground. But light is not there to be admired for its own sake. It is to guide, to make us safer, to scatter the darkness.

- Where are the lights in our communities and nation that are not from the church? How do they illuminate our shared lives?
- What is it that our churches are called to illuminate in our communities?
- What is the darkness that must be scattered?

PART 7

A Beginner's Guide to Beginning Again

18

Beyond Surviving Church

Forgiveness is not about forgetting. It is a fertile, fecund act – one of generative remembering. But nobody can compel another to forgive, and nobody can demand to be reconciled. Forgiveness takes time. It cannot be forced.

Many readers and followers of http://survivingchurch.org – an excellent website, bravely and pastorally curated by Stephen Parsons – will know the pain of sexual abuse first-hand. Others will have walked alongside victims. Others have had to endure the journey of false accusation, Kafkaesque processes and the endless carousel of secret committees. All will have suffered hideously shocking treatment by their bishop, the National Safeguarding Team (NST) or some other ecclesiastical body. The Spanish Inquisition may yet emerge as a more morally decent exemplar of pastoral integrity and justice compared to the Church of England. Give it time. History will judge.

To err is human; to forgive is divine. But though we may pray, 'Forgive us our sins as we forgive those who sin against us', no one can make us forgive. The hurt caused by harm is a wilderness of pain, and you may spend as long in that place as the Israelites spent in the desert. You may have secured freedom from your oppressor, but the oasis and promised lands may take decades to get to.

Nothing anyone can say or write will diminish the pain and suffering of victims. Nor should it. The wounds, hurts, sin and evil need addressing. They are not to be wished away. The gospel is love, but it also conveys tough home truths. Christianity is not a fairy tale with a happy ending.

God's Easter work is the greatest act of forgiveness. Good Friday is packed with violence, travesties of justice, betrayal, desertion, humiliation, cruelty and the banality of evil. It is the wanton rejection and destruction of God's love in Jesus. But Easter – in a springtime garden – is new life, new hope and new starts. All is forgiven. There is no reckoning or retribution. But neither is there forgetting. Jesus is still marked by the violence of Good Friday. He shows those scars to his disciples. Even in his resurrection body. So we can remember.

So how are victims supposed to move forward, marked by Good Friday, yet freed by Easter Sunday? Archbishop Bergoglio of Buenos Aires (1998–2013) – before he became Pope Francis – lived through some of the darkest political times in Argentinian history. The military dictatorships accounted for between 10,000 and 30,000 deaths during the (so-called) Dirty War. Many of the deaths were young men who had been kidnapped, tortured and then killed by the military or police.

These 'Disappeared' remain a national wound and an irrevocable indictment – a scar on the culture of the time. Bergoglio's writings from that time made an important distinction between sin and corruption. In distinguishing the two, he suggests sin and corruption call for very different responses. Sins, argued Bergoglio, were more singular acts that need not be self-perpetuating. Corruption, on the other hand, though clearly connected to sin, and resulting from sins committed and repeated over time, evolves to become a culture in its own right.

In Peter Drucker's famous maxim, 'culture eats strategy for breakfast'. Daringly, Bergoglio suggested that while sin could be forgiven, corruption should not be. Bergoglio held that at the root of corruption was the refusal of God's forgiveness – because the corrupted person, institution or organization denies the need for repentance and, with that, correction. The body that refuses to repent believes it is near-perfect. Or perhaps worse, must maintain the appearance of that perfection. This is why we grind our teeth every time a government minister or prime minister refuses to ever say sorry.

Likewise, bishops are exactly the same when they say they will do better with safeguarding, or announce another review, or try and distract and dilute the deep, boiling anger of victims with some other new initiative. Corruption, unless named, acknowledged and corrected, only grows – like a slow cancer.

Those who – it must be said, usually unwittingly – become the guardians of such systems of abusive culture have forgotten their shared humanity and Christianity. Far from being earthenware vessels containing the treasure of the gospel, the corrupted become hard of heart, and hardened to the hurt they continue to cause. In protecting their reputations, power, privilege, status or wealth, their hearts and the treasure they guard become entwined.

To conceal this entrapment and enslavement, a culture of corruption will often energetically cultivate an appearance of righteousness and civility. Those caught up in this, justifying themselves, finally become convinced of their own moral superiority. They will never apologize.

In contrast, a sinner (even when not ready to repent) will usually have sufficient self-awareness to know they are a sinner. They will know something of the taste of the quality of mercy, and will ask for forgiveness. In so doing, they will be open to grace. The corrupt, by denying their sin, and believing with pride in their own sanctity and superiority, spurn and close down the possibility of grace.

So while sin can be forgiven, Bergoglio argued that corruption must be treated and cured. Here, in terms of corruption, churches are at their most dangerous and vulnerable. Those guarding or perpetuating their own cultures of corruption will eventually engage in 'dialogue' – on gender, sexuality and safeguarding for example – and may even grant you some concessions. This only serves to feed their sense of worth, and might even help them believe that they are genuinely accommodating and perhaps even a bit sorry. But in fact they are not. They do not want to lose their power and privilege. They cannot say sorry. They cannot repent.

What happens next is even more dangerous for institutions. A kind of cancer-like 'purity spiral' will develop. The drivers of the oppressive culture cannot believe that they are participating in and perpetuating any wickedness or cruelty. They are, after all, not bad people. But they have become hard-wired into the culture, and they defend it as they might the gospel.

At this point, even the most passive agents in the abusive culture will work harder and harder to disassociate themselves from any suggestion of being impure, wicked or offensive. It is at this point the authority of the church to preach forgiveness is profoundly compromised by the sexual abuse crisis. The church loses its moral bearings. It cannot tell other people that sins must be forgiven when it cannot see that its own culture remains intact and will continue to abuse.

Bishops may say they are sorry for another abusive, botched or suppressed 'lessons learned' review. But without repentance and condemnation, the pattern of abuse and cover-ups continues. If the corrupt culture is not going to be changed, then you can forgive as many sins as you like. It will make no difference to previous, current and future victims.

As Bergoglio observed, Jesus does cure the corrupt. Yet not through acts of mercy, but rather through engineering major trials and the deliberate infliction of disturbing trauma. In Luke 8, Jairus is made to wait for Jesus to heal his daughter. Jesus, running late, and quite deliberately so, does nothing to prevent her untimely death. But in the act of healing the woman with continuous menstrual bleeding, he enables her to participate in synagogue worship once again. She is healed. Her stigmatization is taken away by Jesus' touch. No longer impure, she has her status restored.

Jairus, a synagogue ruler, would have been instrumental in excluding this woman from such worship. The healing of the woman, and the raising of Jairus' daughter, is both a blessing and a trauma for Jairus. It is bitter-sweet. For Jairus must now face the culture of exclusion he was instrumental in upholding. He must face this woman. To get Jairus to this point, he is arguably made to lose and grieve for his daughter. She dies. The moral lesson of the miracle lies in the judgement it makes against the culture of exclusion in ritual purity. Only when the culture is exposed to trauma can it change. Jairus may now repent. But it will be the trauma of his loss that got him there.

Such traumas have the potential to pierce the armour of corruption and allow grace to enter. To treat faith as a suit of armour – a means of self-defence – is to deny the possibility of God surprising us with amazing grace, the compassion of the stranger and the revelation of Christ in the prisoner, hungry, sick and homeless. If we encase ourselves in our own armoured personal faith, we will only mummify ourselves. But never enough, so our body soon degrades and decomposes. The body that we armour too tightly becomes pallid, compromised, corrupted, and eventually stinks.

Throughout the Gospels, we see Jesus *not* forgiving the sins of the scribes, Pharisees and Sadducees. Their culture is a bellwether indicator of a religion that regards itself as morally self-sufficient and superior to others. Jesus' caustic castigations – straining gnats while swallowing camels, or picking out specks in someone else's eye when there is a plank in your own – are *unforgiving*.

Those who are corrupt will always try and justify themselves with comparisons to others. The parable of the Pharisee and sinner in the Gospel of Luke (chapter 18) comes to mind, with its hints of smug triumphalism. In safeguarding, we find this in announcements and speeches at General Synod: 'We have set up an Independent Safeguarding Board' recently comes to mind. The gullible are fooled, but victims of abuse and shockingly bad process are not, for the culture is the same, and remains intact and immune to true change.

The Church of England's safeguarding culture ensures that all power differentials remain in place, including secrecy, unsafe and unlawful processes. With the ISB, once again the Church of England's culture of corruption has sired a body that has no accountability, scrutiny, fairness, transparency or external regulation. We find the same fear-driven self-sufficiency baked in with moral superiority. This is corrupt.

Yet in the parable of the Pharisee and sinner, the latter articulates not only their guilt but also their sense of shame. In contrast, the corrupt will usually be triumphantly, shamelessly and morally smug. Moreover, the agents of this culture of corruption can easily recruit more accomplices, as they are offering them an experience of graduation into moral-spiritual superiority, self-satisfaction and self-sufficiency. This culture eats all nascent initiatives designed to correct it. In the end, it will of course consume itself.

Jesus had to reject the religious elites of his day because they had taken possession of the law and tradition, its meanings and applications. We have an old saying: 'possession is nine-tenths of the law'. By claiming ownership of faith, religion and morality, the religious elites of Jesus' time were able to remain aloof.

These religious leaders could issue edicts. They could decide if and when they went into 'dialogue', and with whom. Most difficult questions could be left unanswered, and difficult questioners were censured and censored. To most victims of safeguarding processes, that is their ongoing experience too: a daily diet of stones, snakes and scorpions from the National Safeguarding Team (NST). There is never any bread.

By purloining religion – in theory to protect it, but in the end to possess it – the religious elites of Jesus' day were able to put themselves above others. The elite were not like the people. Leaders could not be weighed, cross-examined, investigated, inspected or judged. Anyone who joined this elite acquired power and privilege, with immunity from accountability. Here, bishops, the NST and others in power are the direct descendants of Pharisees and Sadducees.

As Pope Francis noted, Jesus, by walking with the poor and outcast, befriending them as valued equals in the kingdom of heaven, simply 'smashed the wall that prevented [them] from coming close to God'. So we are back with the necessity of creative rage and constructive destruction. Why? Because the offer of dialogue by those remaining in power can never heal corruption. The only way to deal with corruption is to cause the powerful serious trials, tribulations and traumas, so that grace can finally break through, light pierce the fog of bureaucracy, and the winds of the Spirit scatter the secrets shrouded in darkness.

Lest there be any doubt about this, remember Jesus' words in Matthew 18.6–7:

> Whoever causes one of these little ones ... to stumble would be better drowned in the depths of the sea, with a great millstone round the neck. Alas for the world that there should be causes of stumbling! Causes of stumbling there must be, but alas for anyone who provides them!

On the face of it, this issue is apparently a 'tripping point'. Romans 14.13 bears that out:

> Let us each stop passing judgement, therefore, on one another and decide instead that none of us will place obstacles in the way of a brother or sister, or trip them up.

A millstone around your neck is a pretty heavy block. Yet our term 'stumbling block' is not what it seems. It comes from the Greek word *skandalon* (used 15 times in the New Testament) and is the source of our word 'scandal'. The corresponding verb, 'to cause to stumble', is *skandalizō* (used 30 times in the New Testament), from which we get our word *scandalize*.

To us moderns, a scandal is just toxic gossip and tabloid tittle-tattle. However, to the ancient Greeks, a scandal was the trigger mechanism for a baited trap. Later, it came to mean the actual trap as a whole, or something that tripped a person up, causing them to stumble and fall. In the Bible, a stumbling block is anything that causes a person to fall – be that into sin, false teaching or unbelief. But there is another side to this. Jesus Christ was a *skandalon*: 'we are proclaiming a crucified Christ: to the Jews a stumbling-block, and to the gentiles foolishness' (1 Corinthians 1.23).

It might surprise you to learn that Pope Francis argued that the merciful response to the corrupt is to place a stumbling-block, a *skandalon*, in their path, which is the only way of forcing them to seriously contemplate taking a different road. One thinks of the rich man who obeys all the law and excels at good works. What else is he to do? A *skandalon* is placed before him. Jesus tells him, 'If you wish to be perfect, go and sell your possessions and give the money to the poor, and you will have treasure in heaven; and come, follow me.' But when the young man heard this statement, he went away grieving, for he owned much property and had enormous wealth (Matthew 19.21–22).

The way to deal with the culture of corruption in the Church of England's safeguarding is to put many *skandalon* in their way. It forces those following these paths to divert and deviate. Eventually it will impede them. Only when they renounce the corruption can they escape and be free. Only then, when there is sorrow, contrition and personal responsibility, can there be confession and forgiveness. Only then can one welcome them back and begin to speak of authentic dialogue, reconciliation and healing.

We know that to be fully alive means having hope and being able to forgive. That means being released from our past burdens and being open to the hope of the future. The Eucharist is a *skandalon* too. It expresses a fearless, daring, brave and defiant hope in the midst of gross injustice, cruelty and violence.

The Eucharist is an audacious act of generosity and grace in the face of these forces of evil that are bent on destruction and death. 'On the night before he died he had supper with his friends.' Obviously that is what everyone does before meeting their end in violent cruel torture and a slow lingering death. Supper. With friends.

The Eucharist is not meant to be a convivial gathering for a meal accompanied by cheerful songs and sentiments. It is the taking of bread, breaking it and sharing it. It is the taking of the cup and sharing it. It is this act of remembrance – even in pre-empting the crucifixion – that we may now gather and share, and know the presence and love of God, despite whatever may come next.

Yet the Jesus who is the true *skandalon* is not the usual Christ that first comes into our minds. Sometimes the expression of passionate anger and acting it out is important, even prophetic. What are we to make of Jesus driving out the money-changers and traders from the Temple precincts, recorded in the Gospel of John (2.13–16)? Jesus creates mayhem in the Temple and upsets all the people going about their lawful trading in dubious religious tat. And he goes the whole hog too, driving them out with a whip that he made himself. Jesus doesn't do things by halves. Jesus' apparent rush of blood to the head in this Temple story, where he not only conducts himself like a teenager in line for an anti-social behaviour order but also goes on to claim the Temple for his own ends. So Jesus' action in the Temple – reckless, violent and apparently intemperate – contains a strong message.

It is a message of wisdom. Breaking oppressive frames of reference requires dramatic action. This is about smashing a culture of corruption. There is really no point trading up from a pigeon to a dove. Neither sacrifice brings you closer to God; both are a waste of your money. There was no point in going for the 'three for two' offer on goats, nor this month's 'buy one get one free' offer on lambs. And this is why Jesus' 'anger' in the Gospel is so interesting. For it seems not to be a hot, quick, irrational 'temper-snap', but rather a cold and calculating anger. There is a difference between hot anger and cold, perhaps righteous anger.

John's Gospel records that Jesus saw what was going on in the Temple. He then left, went away and *made* the whips of cords. Then he returned. This is a cold premeditated attack; not a rush of blood to the head. He has, as the Epistle to James puts it, 'been slow to anger' – but he's got there. This is how to disrupt a corrupt culture. Dialogue won't do. Like Arnold Schwarzenegger as the robot from the future in *The Terminator*, Jesus has seen the Temple, and says, 'I'll be back'.

As Harvey Cox noted in *On Not Leaving It to the Snake* (1968), the first and original sin is not disobedience. It is indifference. We can no longer ignore the pain and alienation that others in the church experience, especially when this is *because* of the church. Indifference is pitiful, and it is the enemy of compassion. The stranglehold of a corrupted culture must be broken.

The scandal of safeguarding in the Church of England is learned indifference; double-standards; strained gnats, then camels swallowed whole; beams and motes; the amount of money spent on process, but not people; the lies, secrecy, double-speak, 'PR and Comms'; the offer of dialogue that leads to no change; picking off victims one by one; endless, slow, treacle-like procedures; gross misconduct; even grosser incompetence; the hypocrisy and the hype.

But I do believe we can get beyond enduring this – yes, beyond surviving church. This can only be done by bringing religious leaders to their knees. Not, initially, for them to be asking for forgiveness. That is for later. Bringing the presiders of safeguarding to their knees is about breaking a corrupt culture with *skandalon*, and these must be financial and reputational.

In Canada, Australia and the USA, denominations with significant histories of abuse only began to repent when the financial consequences became extremely serious. Up until then, it was decades of victims being given the run-around in the search for truth, justice and redress, and the churches (or church schools) going through the gears of non-disclosure agreements, endless reviews, false promises, blaming the past, blaming the victims, and doing this all so very, very slowly. Something has to give. The victims of cruel, unaccountable and indifferent processes came together and litigated. Ultimately, there is always a body liable for such corruption, abuses, harm and cover-ups.

With the Redress Scheme in the Church of England now delayed, diluted and dispersed across dioceses once again, we are increasingly of the view that all the survivors, victims and respondents (also often abused by very bad, incompetent or unlawful processes) will not secure any redress or justice until we bring some kind of class action. Films featuring abuse in the Catholic Church (see *Spotlight*, *Sins of the Father* and related films such as *Dark Waters* and *Erin Brockovich*) chart the plight of the abused who are made to wait years and years for justice.

But as the Roman Catholic Archdiocese of Boston and the Anglican Churches of Australia and Canada found to their (considerable) cost, somewhere in these places, ultimately, there *is* to be found responsibility and liability. This has led to church buildings and church land being sold for redress and compensation. It means victims can finally get the therapeutic care they need, and perhaps investment leading to new work. They can get their legal fees back. And their lives. The falsely accused, drummed out of the church without trial or rights, can feed and house their families.

To get beyond surviving church, victims of sexual abuse and miscarriages of justice in this corrupted safeguarding culture of the Church of England need to work together – to name those who seek to remain nameless and to shine a light on the things still hidden in darkness. The offer of forgiveness and reconciliation only comes when the culture of corruption has been completely smashed to smithereens, repented of, rendered utterly obsolete and finally defeated. That day will surely come. There is little to fear, and much to hope for. But where to begin?

An important step forward for the Church of England will be the complete adoption of the Human Rights Act 1998, the Equality Act 2010, standard employment law, full compliance with Freedom of Information requests and legislation on data (GDPR), and underpinned by the seven 'Nolan Principles' for conduct in public life. These principles are:

1 Selflessness
2 Integrity
3 Objectivity
4 Accountability
5 Openness
6 Honesty
7 Leadership.

The Seven Principles of Public Life provide a framework of integrity for institutions. Universities, schools, hospitals, county councils, government and other public bodies have adopted them. The ethical standards set out in the Nolan Principles were a response to various scandals in public and parliamentary life under the government of John Major. This included misconduct that might not have been technically illegal, but was nonetheless regarded as corrupt and self-serving. Those working in the public sector are expected to adhere to these standards. They were originally set out by Lord Nolan in 1995 in the first report of the Committee on Standards in Public Life and are now standard in a range of codes relating to proper conduct across public life.

Yet these are nowhere to be found in the Church of England, where secrecy, conflicts of interest, favouritism, obfuscated processes and self-protection reign untrammelled. Without any external regulation – the Church of England is virtually 'a law unto itself' – human rights, basic employment rights and other protections for clergy and laity are simply not present. True, many of the examples of misconduct are innocent mistakes that then get covered up and go unaddressed; for example, complaints procedures and investigations in which the complainant is not interviewed or consulted, but told (eventually), 'There is nothing to see here.'

If the Church of England seeks to be a public body in the present and future, then it will have to model a level of fairness, justice, equality, accountability, transparency and integrity that at present it shows no sign of wishing on itself. Bishops and their staff can do as they please to whomsoever they please (within reason), and there are few, if any, internal mechanisms within the Church of England to bring them to account. This only fosters a culture resistant to openness, honesty and objectivity. Their mercurial and monarchic decisions can rarely be challenged. Perhaps the only way forward will be to regulate the Church of England in order to prevent abuses of power and authority. The alternative is to not regard it as a public body and allow it to slowly deflate into becoming a members-based sect.

More personally, I recall – several years ago – being very surprised to receive a call, out of the blue, from a non-English diocese thanking me for my interest in the vacant See and inviting me to interview. They had received my paperwork from Lambeth Palace and were keen to progress this. But nobody at Lambeth Palace had asked (a) can they forward my data, (b) was I willing to explore this See, and (c) did I feel called to this place? The subsequent phone call with the Appointments Secretary did not improve the emerging picture. Apparently, I could toddle off to this other diocese and come back to the Church of England in a few years' time (again, no sense of calling or vocation). Had Lambeth Palace thought about my wife's work, my children, our life in general, or current vocation? No. Furthermore, any attempts on my part to try and explain the dynamics of prayerful vocation to some ecclesiocrat manager only fluent in management-speak were simply hopeless.

It is well known, especially by those who are suffering with incurable conditions, that sometimes giving up hope leads to unexpected release and joy. The loss of hope, or a deliberate parting with it, is seldom done in an instant. It happens over time as we struggle for any and all routes to what we hope for. But giving up hope is not necessarily an act of despair. It can be creative and freeing. In giving up hope of a miracle recovery from imminent death (your own, or someone else's), or of some other amazing cure, we embrace our identity and learn to live with and accept what we have and what we are.

This is the essence of C. S. Lewis's *Surprised by Joy*. His acceptance of the tragic loss of his wife and ensuing grief helped him rediscover joy. In so doing, he found his way back to gratitude and grace. So letting go of hope can be a pathway to joy. But let me also say that hopelessness is a freedom and position few possess, because it only works if there is a safety net that can save you from utter despair. Those grieving, or living with chronic conditions or degenerative disabilities or, for that matter, the scars of abuse need to be loved, supported and held as much as any other person. You can depart in peace from what you had yearned and hoped for, but only if there is enough hope and joy around you to sustain you in your identity, and with the experiences of loss, pain, trauma and trial that you carry.

This opens up other fronts that we might want to reflect

on. One thinks of the infectious joy and laughter of Desmond Tutu, and his joy in those around him, that became a singular and disarming weapon against hatred, bitterness and oppression. One thinks of the joy in church services that carry us forward in our journeys of hope. Come to think of it, where we find a lack of joy, we often find little to hope for.

Here, I think of the extraordinary group of survivors and victims that I have been privileged – and it is a privilege – to be part of since 2016. They welcome others into their fold. They hate injustice. They can sometimes despair. They look out for each other, and when one is very, very down, and senses all is hopeless, others in the group will pick that person up. The flame of hope is never extinguished. But more than that, this group knows joy. They take delight in each other's company, milestones, weekend plans, meals out (tweeted), pets, partners and holiday plans.

Present and preaching at a service of Evensong in May 2020, I noted this group's amazing 'vibe': 15 per cent grit; 15 per cent comedy club and 70 per cent French Resistance. It is amazing how sustaining joy is, because its presence is a mark of resilience and its absence a confirmation of desolation, defeat and despair. You cannot fake joy. It must be authentic. Because it must be grounded in the lightness of our being and the utter capacity to delight in others. Humour can be part of this, as much as tears of joy. But note, this is all berthed in the deep-water harbour of kindness. And it is from those depths that, sometimes, the kindest and best thing to do is to make Jairus wait, or make a scene in the courts of the Temple with the hawkers and tat-merchants. There is the good kind of anger and passionate rage (for justice) that flows from love and wants to see joy, peace and hope for all.

So, in conclusion, what is to be done about the Church of England and its wretched, self-perpetuating litany of excuses for safeguarding? As the saying goes, 'Don't get mad, get even.' These rough places need levelling, the path straightening and the oppressed raising up. This must necessitate a very different approach to the current impasse.

This corrupt culture will be broken. There is no one path that brings about change. Protests, publishing and picketing are important. Not giving up, ever, is vital. Sticking together is essential. But perhaps the biggest difference to be made for change lies in law and litigation. Because God loves righteousness. And God loves the law and the justice and redemption it brings. Law is also the third party in the diatribes and disputes about responsibility and liability. This is the lesson of King Solomon and his wisdom. A third party making the decisions, judgements and issuing a definitive ruling is the place where disputes can end, and the litigants let go and be free to find joy.

As long as the Church of England evades its lawful responsibilities in safeguarding, the joy will continue to drain away from the office of bishop. At the same time, the hope in that office will evaporate. But the settlement must be significant, and of a proportion that signals a genuine act of deep, permanent repentance. The settlement cannot leave the perpetrators in power. Nor can it leave the structures in place. To repent, these must be set aside – for ever.

The sums of money that will work for comprehensive redress will be in the nine figure range. But when all is said and done, £100 million is less than 1 per cent of the wealth of the Church Commissioners. If the Church of England is serious about redress, those who pave the way in a class action on behalf of others should probably argue for that final number to be a whole tithe of the Church Commissioners' wealth. Or, the Church of England could simply take out another loan. Just as there was a recent £550 million 'Sustainability Bond' for the Church of England, so there must now be a 'Redress and Reconciliation Bond'.

After all, victims will still be coming forward for the first time in the decades ahead. This means taking on the body that is ultimately responsible for the gross negligence, indifference, obfuscation, misconduct, corruption and other failings we see all the time in safeguarding. The fund will need to be very, very large, carefully set up, completely out of the hands of the church, and able to compensate, support and help other victims in the future yet to emerge. That is a major work, and it will require major funding.[1]

The long-running independent public statutory inquiry established to examine the circumstances in which men, women and children treated by the NHS in the UK were given infected blood and infected blood products is now nearing its end. The Hillsborough victims took years to get the justice that they sought for those who lost their lives. That is the journey we are now on with victims of safeguarding and abuse in the Church of England. Only when the journey ends can there ever be closure. When we arrive at that terminus, there will be peace and joy. And new hope.

Note

1 https://www.cityam.com/exclusive-uk-becomes-europes-leading-jurisdiction-for-class-action-lawsuits/ (accessed 21.1.2022).

19

Plentiful Redemption

It was Oscar Wilde who, while attending a particularly boring party, was asked by his host if he was enjoying himself. 'Of course,' retorted Wilde, 'there is nothing else to enjoy.' Jesus was present at a few parties and seems to have enjoyed himself. In fact it seems that for some Jesus enjoyed himself rather too much (Luke 7.33–34). Nor was the choice of company he kept too popular. As well as going to parties, Jesus used them in his parables, most notably in the parable of the great feast (Luke 14.16–24). In the story Jesus told, someone is throwing a party, to which he invites many guests. The guests he has invited will not come, giving a variety of excuses, so the host sends slaves out into the streets to bring in the beggars and the lame, and when there is still room (perhaps they too gave excuses not to come to the party) he sends his slave out again to the roads outside the city. The slave is told to forget about inviting people to the party, and just compel people to come.

A parable cannot be exhausted by one telling, one sermon or one meaning. Parables have an interpretative range. There is something about the way in which they can be told and retold, and different things will crop up in each telling. The essence of a good parable, like the essence of a good party, will sometimes lie in complete *excess*. The art of listening to parables, as opposed to the art of telling them, is the art of placing oneself in the story-world they create. It is this connection between our world and the world of the parable that makes them such a powerful means of communication.

Many of the parables that Jesus tells are about things that are thrown away, used up or finished with. Whether it be a banquet that is eaten, seed that is being thrown around (note, only a quarter of which is ultimately productive) or salt dug into the ground, Jesus' subjects, like Jesus himself, are used and then disposed of. This excess is exuberance to the point of wastefulness. So many of Jesus' parables give us stories of absurd, overwhelming abundance at no cost. Parables point us to God. Parables invite us, the reader, inside. Just as a host invites us to a lunch, dinner or party, we need to RSVP and then attend. Yet when we arrive we do often find ourselves in a situation and position we had not anticipated.

So, where do we place ourselves in the parable of the great feast? One understanding of the story is that it is a Christian party (cold quiche and warm fellowship?). Those invited are the Jews, but once they refuse the invitation, God (the host) sends his slave to compel others (Christians) to come in. The church seems to have misunderstood its role in the parable. Far from a controlling position, the church may find itself in the position of being among those originally invited. The feast of Jesus' story is not a Christian party, but God's party – an important distinction. We may find that, as Christians, we are rather amazed at the people God has invited to the kingdom party, and that we are just a handful among the many. In fact the chief danger is that we might not turn up to God's party at all, having found something better or more worthy to do. Worst of all, we might grumble about those whom God has invited, in much the same way that Jesus' contemporaries complained about the kind of company he kept.

The parable of the labourers in the vineyard (Matthew 20.1–16) drives home this point with blunt-force impact. 'That's not *fair*!' is a wail that nearly every parent dreads but knows only too well. Children develop a very keen sense of injustice early on, especially when their own deserts are at stake. In a society that is conscious of fairness through workplace disputes, strikes, picketing, payment and differentials, waiting lists, public anger about fat cats and inflated bonuses, there is a lot of unfairness. Surely in a just society rewards should be distributed according to merit and pay related to work? It would appear in this parable that the complainants have a very strong case, and most members of any church congregation would agree with them. But as with nearly all of Jesus' parables, there is more to the story than meets the eye.

Clearly, the vineyard is a workplace. In Palestine, as with other agrarian economies, the window for harvest is short, and in particular the grape harvest comes just after a season of heavy rain. So the vineyard owner needs the maximum number of workers for the minimum amount of time. The workers themselves are day labourers – the most insecure, powerless and exploited of all, they are hired by the day and paid at sunset. Thus an idle day is a hungry day. The wages described in the parable are only just enough for a family to live on.

The parable introduces some surprises even before we get to the end. As the sun sets, the labourers line up for their pay, and this is where the trouble really begins. For a start, the men who were hired last are paid first, but to their great surprise they get a full day's wage. Those who have been at work all day rub their hands with anticipated glee: obviously they're going to get a day's work and a bonus! But they don't. It is the same wage for everyone, irrespective of how hard they have worked. No wonder the cry comes, 'That's not fair.' So what does this parable of apparent unfairness mean?

One standard way of interpreting the parable was to focus on the equality of pay. In other words, the vineyard owner is acting mercifully by making sure that all have enough money to feed and clothe their family. John Ruskin's exposition of the parable was an eloquent attack on the economic theory of his day. Ruskin was an associate of F. D. Maurice and Charles Kingsley, and they were very committed to early Christian socialism. Ruskin, in his exhortation, pleads for a sort of minimum wage, describing the parable as offering a pattern for the Christian care of the underprivileged and the powerless. Whatever you think of that interpretation, it certainly has some merit.

Yet there are deeper meanings in the parable that lie even beyond this social and political exposition. In this respect, it is useful to distinguish between what is fair and what is generous, and the relation between earnings and needs. The parable makes a delightful play on our own childish conceptions of fairness in relation to the vineyard, which I take to be a cipher for the kingdom of God. The parable sketches out the generosity of God as being so abundant that it is, in the end, deeply *unfair*.

In other words, here is a parable that questions our motivations and our reasoning. The parable is aimed at the sort of people whose conscious rectitude makes it difficult for them to allow God to be generous to those who have done less well. Do we really feel that we have 'earned' God's favour? Invariably many do. This is the English fondness for the Pelagian heresy: God is running a secret rewards-bonus-card scheme for loyal followers. The more you expend, the more you earn. To characterize English Pelagianism, you can't actually attain salvation but, by working harder for God, you can get some extra club-card benefits that other folk don't bother with.

Here – again – we have a parable that sides with the lazy, the publicans and sinners, those who have done less well and worked less hard. Maybe that is opportunity, class, social demographics or health. The parable does not explain why there are some people who are the last to be picked to work, but you don't need much imagination to figure it out.

Illegal workers picked up in lines and ferried in trucks and buses from one poor country to work over the border in their richer neighbouring country have several things in common with the labourers in this parable. The gangmasters pick the strongest, healthiest and most compliant, those who won't complain and will not be members of a union or bleat for workers' rights. If desperate, the gangmasters might have to make do with slower, older and less fit workers. But nobody with a harvest to gather will pick the lame, disabled, elderly, slow – or those who might complain, or need medical support to just get through the day. Labourers are chosen on the basis that they won't argue, and have no needs – save only that they will do anything for the wage at the end of the day.

As now, so then. Jesus is describing an exploited but also fit and compliant workforce, who, as the day progresses, find that all their hard work risks being undermined by people less fit and doubtless less good at the work. In turn, that may have an impact on the brightest and very best labourer and what they are deemed to be worth in terms of wages. If the lame, maimed, blind, deaf and dumb are now picking the crops, supported by those with an assortment of mental incapacities and disabilities, there will be serious issues of quality control. So the pay-out flagged at the end – no dividend is given to those who have shouldered the responsibility, borne the heat of the day and done most of the work, and doubtless covered, corrected and compensated the mistakes made by the poor, rather hopeless workers. It is shocking, if not scandalous. Put yourself in the shoes of the ones who have done the most work in terms of quantity and the best in terms of quality: you are going to be paid the same as the slackers and hopeless, those that no employer in their right mind would ever take on.

The parable is of course a sharp, fierce, sarcastic criticism of the religion of Jesus' day and our churches now. God's love is not rationed. It is not apportioned according to ability, worth, merit, class or graft. Nobody gets more of God's love as a result of their genes, heritage, effort, intelligence or achievement. That is salvation: love's redeeming work is done. In the war between Jesus and the church, the church is ahead on points, but it is a war it cannot win. God will open his kingdom to whom he chooses; all are invited. The church is not the gatekeeper.

The Gospels offer extreme case studies. The dying thief on the cross is an obvious example. He could not have worked in the vineyard for more than a few seconds, let alone an hour, yet on the cross, for the most minimal confession, he is promised paradise. Had the disciples still been around to witness this exchange shortly before the death of Jesus they must have wondered to themselves what on earth the point of giving up everything and forsaking all for the kingdom of God had been. Had they not been with Jesus for three years? Had they not abandoned their jobs? Had they not left behind their families, even leaving the dead unburied? Of course they had. So how is Jesus offering precisely the same – no more and no less – to a man who has been committed to a lifetime of violence and crime? It isn't fair, is it?

The parable gets right under the skin of the real motivation for being part of the church and following Jesus. The interesting thing that the parable suggests is that in Christ's scheme of salvation, the rewards and bonuses scheme is as flat as a heavily ironed pancake. Salvation does not come in half measures or other fractions. You cannot be half saved. You are welcome in God's kingdom. The church is not Border Force Patrol for Jesus; nor is it Immigration Control or an Asylum-Seeking Detention Centre. You can't be half ordained. Salvation is not available in fractions. You cannot be half baptized. You either receive the bread of life and the cup of salvation or you can refuse it, but these 'tokens' of God are not graded according to any reward scheme. They are tokens of free, unmerited grace.

The underlying equality built into this parable also bears one further interpretation, namely God's scant regard for our divisions, categories and labelling. God only sees humans who are loved completely. Humans divide according to class, ability, ethnicity, disability, fitness, intelligence and more besides. This impacts how we value labour too. In an age of cancel culture and toxic social media, we need to remember God has no favourites.

The internet gives us access to information as never before. It enables all kinds of good networking. Yet it also creates mutually reinforcing silos of sentiment, information and opinion. It percolates and intensifies opinion. As shared knowledge declines in value, and partisan opinion and alternative facts reign freely, a new kind of social-civil war has taken root. It allows us to believe – you, me and everyone else – that if we lose an argument, civilization itself is lost, and all we hold to be sacred and cherished will be destroyed.

In one sense, the parable does destroy one cherished world view: that the harder you work, the more you earn. The parable flips this on its head, and says that when it comes to the kingdom of God, and the love of God, the undeserving and the very deserving get all of God's love, equally. Speaking personally, I am very, very happy with that. I think it is the gospel. But I know a lot of Christians who, while agreeing that it is the gospel, begrudge it.

So the parable of the labourers haunts the church and spooks the 'strongest' Christians. (NB: 'strong Christian' is normally a self-description adopted by those who seem so sure of their own righteousness. They are wrong of course, but you'll get nowhere arguing with them. Try praying for them, and slowly converting them through endless acts of kindness and generosity towards others.) The better way to live is to avoid policing the borders and the boundaries of God's kingdom. Don't for a moment entertain the slightest thought that God is interested in any 'Build the Wall' religion to keep some people out. Or that keeping those who are desperate to find a home and salvation in your space need to be stopped in their tracks and turned back to where they came from before they even reach your shore. That might be some dog-whistle politics for insiders, but God is always looking out for the interests of the true outsiders: the unseen, unheard, unknown, undesirable and unemployable. That is undeniable.

The church has no role in checking passports, visa restrictions or immigration control. God's kingdom is not ours to run, let alone police. Instead, we are invited to gather up everybody – as many as we can – to share in precisely the same bounty all of us already enjoy and have known for years.

This parable of the labourers is gospel truth – but bad news for the church. For it points to the foolish abundance, the ridiculous generosity of God in relation to those on whom he bestows his favour. Mercy and grace are infinite, and all shall receive the same. It is the same salvation for the church warden who has put 50 years of hard graft, blood, sweat and tears into keeping a church going as it is for the tiniest child commended to God, who has barely taken one breath before passing away and been scooped up into heaven. Or those in the middle, like you and me, who stumble around in their half belief, perhaps even barely caring about the inheritance that has been bestowed upon us. In all of that, this parable asks, do you rejoice at God's overwhelming abundance, or seek to ration and control it? We can't be saying 'no' to anyone yet – because God's 'yes', his invitation to all, is still there. As F. W. Faber's surprisingly inclusive early Victorian hymn celebrates:

> There's a wideness in God's mercy,
> like the wideness of the sea.
> There's a kindness in his justice,
> which is more than liberty.
>
> There is no place where earth's sorrows
> are more felt than up in heaven;
> there is no place where earth's failings
> have such kindly judgement given.
>
> For the love of God is broader
> than the measure of man's mind,
> and the heart of the Eternal
> is most wonderfully kind.
>
> But we make his love too narrow
> by false limits of our own;
> and we magnify his strictness
> with a zeal he will not own.
>
> There is plentiful redemption
> through the blood that has been shed;
> there is joy for all the members
> in the sorrows of the Head.
>
> There is grace enough for thousands
> of new worlds as great as this;
> there is room for fresh creations
> in that upper home of bliss.

> If our love were but more simple
> we should take him at his word;
> and our lives would be all gladness
> in the joy of Christ our Lord.

If we want to see our churches and denominations, as the body of Christ, comprehensively redeemed in our lifetime, we need some apposite and rigorous revolutions: root and branch. That may well mean resisting and removing those presently in power: 'preparing the way of the Lord' and 'making the path straight'. It may mean an ecclesiastical 'levelling up' and 'levelling down'. (We have had a religious reformation led by Levellers before – nearly 400 years before Boris Johnson appropriated the phrase.) But this will not be a revolution of violence or destruction, or one that is berthed in some violent hate-fuelled agenda. This revolution will be disruptive, for sure, but also constructive. We are meant to be committed to the kingdom of God being built, not recruiting members to some Church Preservation Society.

This revolution must begin with God's love for everyone. We must relearn the lesson: the biggest problem facing the church is coping with the overwhelming abundance of God. Once grasped, the churches will be turned inside out. Only then will the world be turned upside down.

20

Coda

In our age, we might suggest a modest revision to Paul's saying found in 1 Corinthians 10.23: 'All things are permissible, but virtually nothing is forgivable.' In a world turbo-charged by social media and driven by instant accusation, deep suspicion and hate-fuelled hostilities, many walk with wariness, fearful and fretful of mistakes they might make. As many know to their cost, social media has a better memory than a herd of elephants in a conclave. Nothing is forgotten.

In a culture easily influenced by shrill tribalism, it is important to remember that it is hard to divide the sheep and the goats, the wheat from the tares, or the good from the bad. Our society is not well served by sharp divisions: conservative vs liberal; Leavers vs Remainers (be it Europe, the UK or just the Anglican Communion again); victims vs perpetrators; deniers vs believers – the list goes on. True, we can say for the sins of our forebears – slavery, racism, exploitation, anti-Semitism – but this can risk becoming the cheapest trinkets of grace if not matched by our readiness to right the present and set the moral compass for a fairer future.

The scriptures teach us wisely if we can but pause to understand the lessons to be learned. The good Samaritan is good because he does not perform his moral act with any expectation or hope of thanks. His goodness is for goodness' sake. There are no likely beneficial consequences or potential rewards for his actions. Jesus heals ten lepers. One does return to give thanks, but all ten get the same healing, liberation and deliverance from an affliction that rendered them socially isolated and so shunned by all who might merely pass them by.

CODA

As I was reflecting on this coda, and the right note of hope on which to end, a message dropped into my inbox from a young woman whom we welcomed into our home at Christmas some years back. Sherine (not her real name) had been bombed out of a Syrian city. She was (and is) an academic, and through some hard graft we were able to find her some funding to continue with her career. We found a position for her husband too. It was financially challenging, but friends, colleagues and supporters pitched in.

At Christmas, we found ourselves gathered around a table of friends, family and strangers, and managed to contact her family via the internet. All were scattered to different countries, so could not be together. None had a passport, so were stuck where they were, and stateless. It was unclear when – or if – this family would ever be together again. Yet the conversation around the table was filled with gratitude, hope and mutual acts of hospitality.

Sherine and her family had not celebrated Christmas before. They are Muslim. But it has not stopped them, ever, not once, writing from time to time to say that they hold us in prayer and give thanks for just a short season of food, shelter and work. Sherine now lives and works in our country, and her family are flourishing in their careers and respective countries. She wrote to tell me that after seven long years, the family had finally gathered in person.

There is only one valid response for sharing Christmas with those who have nothing to share and nobody to share that with. Good deeds are done for their own sake. Not for reward, reputation or reciprocation. Goodness, like hope, stands alone. The gift of goodness may lead to no results at all. No thanks whatsoever. No acknowledgement, even. There are no surviving records of polite 'thank you' cards and letters addressed to Jesus after the feeding of the 4,000, the 5,000, or for that matter any of the several dozen that he heals. One or two express gratitude. Mostly they don't.

Goodness does not have an end result in mind when it is offered. The moral value, indeed Christian virtue, of being good (that is, active goodness) carries no reward and cannot even assume it results in anything at all. You can take God for granted. You can take grace for granted. You can take goodness and blessings for granted. And God will still love you as though you were the only person left on earth. God would still die for you.

The church needs to recover its mission as a Good Body. Good for others, not because it might be missional, or help the congregations get a few more bums on seats. Pure goodness will do. The more we concentrate on the total rightness and truth of being good, the less the results matter at all.

In this short book I have tried to prise open the stone that lies across the tomb and help Lazarus – the church – come out, be unbound and feel the warmth of the sun on pallid our flesh. Yes, I know that when Lazarus came forth, the shock of the light must have almost blinded him. And the heat might have been unbearable too. I can understand why the cool, dark and dry tomb might feel safer, and certainly more secure.

Yet to be a people of hope we must be reconciled to being a people of risk. The hope of love, faith, union or liberation, or even death, requires us all to let go. In that moment of surrender, we are momentarily lost and vulnerable. And yet how else can we live? The church, I fear, clings tightly to its declining life. It has taken on slogans and mantras, and made them into a litany for loyalists. But this is not the way of Jesus. True teaching opens our eyes, and will for a moment temporarily blind us, or render us stupefied. Of course, blind fundamentalism is appealing in place of such risk. It offers the security, sanctity and safety of no-risk belief. That is why a precarious church is no bad thing. The incarnation itself was precarious at every stage.

The only way through our world's current predicaments is to think harder, hope harder still, and love more than ever. These things are good for their own sake. They are not another Mission Avenue to try and, if we don't like the results or cannot find any, to be set aside. Our journey now is set on recovering a hope-filled world, in which love, joy, patience and peace can flourish; where kindness, self-control and gentleness are the new normal. The ground for that hope is the foundation of Jesus. His life, death, resurrection and ascension proclaim the overwhelming abundance of God – boundless grace, mercy and love – for all. In other words, good news – the gospel.

Reflections for Part 7

> Blessed are those who hunger and thirst for righteousness, for they shall be filled. Blessed are the merciful, for they shall receive mercy. (Matthew 5.6–7)

Size matters. But not to God in the way you might think. His eye is on the fallen sparrow, and counting the number of (remaining?) hairs on your head. The writing of Julian of Norwich (1342–1416) has made a deep impression on me. When she was 30 years old, Julian contracted a grave illness and came so near death they gave her last rites. At the end of her illness, she had several visions, or *shewings*, which she understood to have come from God. She spent the next 20 years reflecting on these visions and writing them down. Perhaps, the most famous of those *shewings* is this one:

> And in this he showed me a little thing, the quantity of a hazel nut, lying in the palm of my hand, as it seemed. And it was as round as any ball. I looked upon it with the eye of my understanding, and thought, 'What may this be?' And it was answered generally thus, 'It is all that is made.' I marvelled how it might last, for I thought it might suddenly have fallen to nothing for littleness. And I was answered in my understanding: It lasts and ever shall, for God loves it. And so have all things their beginning by the love of God. This little thing which is created seemed to me as if it could have fallen into nothing because of its littleness. In this little thing I saw three properties. The first is that God made it. The second that God loves it. And the third, that God keeps it. (Julian of Norwich, *Revelations of Divine Love*, 2015, pp. 7–8)

Sometimes all you can do is look after the small things. Remember, God numbers the hairs on your head. God knows each sparrow that falls.

Small things build up, eventually, into the kind of loving change of culture that can transform the world. Emma Percy's poem 'Blessed are the Meek' captures the beauty and simplicity of the Beatitudes, and what they invite us to dwell upon:

Thank heavens for gentle folk,
the meek and the good.

Who treat others with love and kindness
Who welcome all with open-mindedness
Who hold lightly to this world's wealth
Who cultivate their spirit's health
Who know how to listen and when to speak
Whose meekness is strength; humble not weak
 Who lighten our load and rejoice in what's right
 Whose generous souls bring us all into light
Who are blessed by God and proclaimed of great worth
These, gentle and faithful, will inherit the earth.

These are small things, as I say. So the first Christians looked after the small and forgotten people: the widows, orphans and poor; those unspoken for. And they treated them not as objects of charity but as their equals. They did this for foreigners, friends, neighbours, slaves, free, male, female, young and old. As Donald MacKinnon once opined, 'The Christian God [has been] endowed imaginatively with the attributes of a human Caesar' (*Philosophy and the Burden of Theological Honesty*, 2011, p. 266). Thus, the church takes on the image of a 'transcendent Caesar' rather than the more fundamentally disruptive calling of embodying the 'vulnerable Nazarene'.

What this means in practice will vary across individuals, congregations and communities. But what can be said is that all Christians are incorporated into Christ's continuing life and witness of abiding love, constant presence and compassionate intercession. Christians are participative in the life of Jesus Christ, and in the vine and the branches. In our own self-emptying, wilful descent and conscious path of humility, we are bound to offer the fruits of God's Spirit as gifts to the world, and as participants in Jesus' ecology of service rather than one of mere self-preserving resistance.

This does not call the church, or individuals or groups within the church, to a life of passive acceptance. Rather, it commits us to a very different vocation, and one that is far more costly. It invites us to contemplate the formation of character in a given community or in the lives of individuals afflicted by persecution. Here, we are not asked to model weakness but meekness.

There is, then, a paradox at the heart of kenosis. It is not a kind of weary stoicism or resignation in the face of the malign forces of fate. It is, rather, an act of determination and resolve; an exercise of deep power from within that chooses – in the example of God in Christ – to limit power and knowledge, but not to limit love. Deep forms of humility will no longer privilege power and knowledge. Rather, these will be set aside in a continuous, wilful and generative life of humility that will place others above the self.

The self-limiting of power and knowledge allows love to both cover and hold those who need it most. Indeed, I think many parents will understand something of this. What the child needs to experience is a parent with *some* power and *some* knowledge, but not too much, or else growth and individuation will be stifled.

This can only be fixed within a paradigm of unconditional love, which seeks to sustain and serve the ones we seek to set free. And only love can do this. As it frees, it binds us. Love can be fierce; just as the Passion is a wilful act of determination, not resignation. Moreover, this love can contain anger, and even make space for disruptive acts of prophetic leadership.

God's power is rooted in relinquishing and transforming. It is not kept or traded: it is given away, free. Human power, typically, takes for its own ends, to maintain and grow itself. God's power, located on a foundation of sacrificial love, hospitality and humility, builds up and is eternal. Human power, based on competition and dominance, is temporal and decays. As Moisés Naim notes in *The End of Power: From Boardrooms to Battlefields*:

> Even as rival states, companies, political parties, social movements, and institutions or individual leaders fight for power as they have done throughout the ages, power itself – what they are fighting so desperately to get and keep – is slipping away.
> Power is also decaying. (2013, pp. 1–2)

As I have remarked before on power in Christian leadership and the formation of character, it is often a complex negotiation of virtues and values with the cultural contingencies and challenges being faced. Mixed into this will be elements of projection, along with fantasy, narcissisms and basic human fragility. Good leadership is often formed through adversities that are stayed from decaying into despair and vengeful self-protection.

Maturity and ripeness, if you think about it, are not only about growth. They are about ageing, shedding and making more room for new ideas, relationships, experiences and responsibilities. Ripeness and growth mean a kind of surrender and self-emptying, this yielding to and acceptance of what God does within us when we say 'yes' like Mary's surrender. As God dwells in us, what is squeezed out are the resistances and negativities that will not permit the Holy Spirit to gestate within us. The self-emptying paradigm that is exemplified in Jesus leads to a humble kind of leadership that serves the other. The meekness and openness is magisterial. The one who reigns does so from a tree. His crown is made of thorns.

We conclude this reflection with this contemporary version of the Beatitudes from the Aramaic original, and translated by Patricia Fresen (although I have added 'mature' to 'ripe' for this adapted version):

When Yeshua saw the crowds, he ascended the mountain; and when he sat down, his disciples came to him. And he spoke to them in his native Aramaic tongue, teaching them and saying:

Mature and ripe are those who find their home in the Spirit;
They shall be attuned to the inner reign of God.

Mature and ripe are those who mourn and weep and grieve for people who are suffering;
They shall be comforted and shall be united inside by love.

Mature and ripe are the gentle;
They shall be open to receive strength from the earth and the universe.

Mature and ripe are those who hunger and thirst for justice;
They shall be encircled by the birth of a new society.

Mature and ripe are the compassionate;
Upon them shall be compassion.

Mature and ripe are those who are consistent in heart;
They shall contemplate God.

Mature and ripe are those who plant peace in each season;
They shall be named the children of God.

Mature and ripe are those who are persecuted for the sake of justice;
The reign of God is in them.

Mature and ripe are you when you are conspired against, dislocated and wrongly labelled as immature for my sake;
No matter where you turn, you will find the Name inscribed in light. It is the sign of prophecy to be persecuted.[1]

REFLECTIONS FOR PART 7

Discussion

- As we think about bread for the world, light of the world and salt for the earth, what is the offering that your church, congregation and ministry makes to your community?
- If your church disappeared tomorrow, what would the community have lost in terms of bread, light and salt?
- As we are all of us thirsting for righteousness, what justice and mercy does your community cry out for? What steps has your church taken to be the grace, mercy and peace of God to your community and the people and places you serve?

Note

1 Patricia Fresen, translation (adapted) of the Beatitudes, https://bridgetmarys.blogspot.com/2017/02/the-beatitudes-as-translated-from.html (accessed 11.11.2022)

Afterword

by the Right Revd Dr Peter Selby

There's only one person who (perhaps) agrees with everything in this book, and that's Martyn Percy; and he may well have changed his mind between writing and publication. But there are very many people (probably including Martyn himself) who have been made to think new thoughts by what they have read here.

Among the intriguing pieces of biblical exposition and social commentary there are many moments of passionate critique. There is much here to remind us of the comment of the late Gerald Hudson who after a couple of years as Principal of the Southwark Ordination Course said: 'When I took the job I thought I was to educate people for ministry in the church as it could be in the future, and that was very scary. I now realize that the job is to educate people for ministry in the church as it already is – and that's much scarier.' In his time as a theological college principal Martyn might well have had similar thoughts; there's much here about the church as the contemporary expression of the Christian movement as it is meant to be – and that's exhilarating. But there's also much that drills down into the documents and the representative utterances of the church as it is – and that is by turns infuriating and depressing.

That combination is what prompts this Afterword, one person's disturbed questioning after reading this material. For the sheer range of topics in which the church's own life and its engagement with the life of society and the world it inhabits is such that 'precarious' becomes almost an understatement.

AFTERWORD

How, I ask myself, is the church to respond adequately to such a wide-ranging critique?

The precariousness of the church is described here not just with depth and learning, but with an authority born of personal experience. My guess is that among those who have read *The Precarious Church* will be many, perhaps even the majority, who have watched with horror and outrage the attacks to which Martyn has been subjected. It has been my privilege to be one of those who during many profound conversations with him during that time have been able to read much of the material evidence of what has been visited upon him, as well as the remarkable resilience with which, in the face of all that, he has kept bitterness at bay. Like many I have not been greatly surprised by the behaviour of the governing body of Christ Church – Henry VIII knew what he was doing and chose a form of structural poison with a very long half-life. Equally, like many, but with the particular perception that comes from having been a diocesan bishop myself, I have found the neglect and even gratuitous cruelty to which Martyn has been subjected from those within the church charged with his pastoral care that frankly would have beggared belief had I not read actual examples.

It would not be a worthy reflection on the perceptive critiques contained within these pages to parade at length my personal sympathy, respect and support for the author. He has at no point presented himself as a 'victim' asking for our pity, though such responses would be what comes naturally to anyone but the most hard-hearted. Rather, he has turned his own experience into an instrument of solidarity with others who in various and differing circumstances have found in the church not the community of sanctuary and support they thought they had a right to expect but rather an agency compounding their distress and adding to their burdens. Since Martyn is among those who have been subjected to safeguarding accusations, it is a particular source of respect to notice that he has shown as much concern as anyone for the survivors of abuse and of the failure of the church to respond adequately to the witness they have borne, and far more than many; it is clear that the processes the church has created have inflicted some grievous harm on those who endure accusations, but it is not at all clear that they have brought any commensurate good to survivors.

If pity and even sympathy would not be adequate responses to the critiques that are addressed to the church in these pages, which are the thoughts and actions which they might provoke and which might more appropriately (to use one of the author's un-favourite words) show a seriousness of intent to take up the challenges they offer? That question is addressed, as are the challenges, to the church in general but have a particular force for those who see themselves as part of its 'liberal' tendency as represented by organizations such as Modern Church.

First and foremost, of course, are the specific issues, a large number of them, that confront the reader on the journey through these pages. There are questions to 'discuss' and 'reflect on' at the end of the chapters; but in the end many of them require a more confrontational response than discussion and reflection. If, to take an example that engages the author's passion with particular force, the attempts to achieve 'growth' are a serious misreading of what these times require, then how and where is the 'growth' culture to be interrupted and who will have the courage and the position of representative authority to articulate a corrective and present a different vision? This book offers a task – perhaps for the Union or perhaps for others – to tabulate the critiques offered here with strategies for campaigning or publishing or recruiting for a different vision. Mercifully those who undertake such a task will also find in this volume not just 'jobs to be done' but some wonderful passages of biblical and doctrinal support for their efforts.

There is then a second focus that has informed my own reflections on this book, one that might seem abstract but which could, on the other hand, provide a fundamental theological foundation for the specific engagements just proposed. I have sometimes entertained the fantasy that in the far-off past, perhaps between day five and day six of creation, a meeting

AFTERWORD

took place between the Divine and the multitude of angelic advisers. When God advanced the proposal to entrust the fulfilment of the ambition to bring into being a world of beauty and flourishing to a community of human beings, most of the angelic advisers had serious doubts, but nobody had the courage to voice them; and so the project went ahead. Had any of them had the courage to critique the intention of entrusting to human beings so important a project, they would have based their objection, surely, not simply on the fickleness and fallibility of individual human agents but primarily on the fact that human beings entrusted with a project invariably create an institution to carry it out – what else could they do? And institutions once created exhibit certain inevitable characteristics: they create boundaries; they raise funds; they make judgements about who should be excluded for bad behaviour. In short, and often with the best of intentions, they end up prioritizing the needs of the institution itself over the objectives for which they were created in the first place, and have the capacity to justify even the most egregious departures from the behaviour to be expected from those who profess Christian faith by reference to institutional needs and various versions of institution-speak.

What we have read here has a background and foreground. In the background, acknowledged in the Preface, lie precisely some of those most egregious departures from Christian norms of which Martyn has been on the receiving end. In the foreground, the important critiques of aspects of the church's institutional life which form the content of the succeeding chapters. Those critiques require reflection and debate, the virtues of wisdom and careful analysis. That is not what is needed in relation to the experiences that constitute the background to those critiques: they require confrontation, courage, solidarity and the single-minded pursuit of justice and repentance.

The distinction is critical. If we respond to critiques of institutional life with an immediate adoption of campaign mode, we are likely to imagine we can leap straight from the jubilee manifesto uttered by Christ in the Nazareth synagogue to demands for change which do not take seriously the complexities that are inextricably bound up with the church's existence as an institution within a complicated and changing social order. But if we respond to what are clearly acts of oppression and injustice by allowing the powers that shape the institution to obfuscate with excuses of complexity, we shall avoid the challenge to our courage and solidarity and fail those who need us most.

There is in these pages a summons to a demanding discernment: for those whose instinct is to campaign, a requirement to engage with the complexities of institutional life; and for those who more readily undertake precisely the hard work of that engagement, the call of injustice to resist.

Peter Selby
Formerly Bishop of Worcester and Bishop to HM Prisons

References and Further Reading

Applebaum, Anne, 2013, conversation with Roger Scruton, 6 June 2012, in *The Iron Curtain*, London: Allen Lane.
Augustine, *The Works of Saint Augustine: A Translation for the 21st Century*, trans. and notes Edmund Hill, ed. John E. Rotelle, Brooklyn, NY: New City Press, 1990.
Ballard, J. G., 1962, *The Drowned World*, New York: Berkley Books.
BBC, 2019, *Editorial Guidelines*, 2019, www.bbc.com/editorialguidelines/guidelines (accessed 7.11.2022).
Chang, Jung, 2003, *Wild Swans*, London: Collins.
Church Growth Conference, 1987, *Christianity Today Magazine*, July 1987.
Clegg, Stewart, 1979, *The Theory of Power and Organizations*, London and Boston, MA: Routledge and Kegan Paul.
Cox, Harvey, 1968, *On Not Leaving It to the Snake*, London: SCM Press.
Dulles, Avery, 1976, *Models of the Church*, Dublin: Gill and Macmillan.
Field, Frank, 1987, *The Politics of Paradise: A Christian Approach to the Kingdom*, London: Fount.
Gerlach, Luther P. and Virginia H. Hine, 1970, *People, Power, Change: Movements of Social Transformation*, New York: Bobbs-Merrill.
Gibbs, Eddie, 1981, 'The Relevance of Church Growth Principles to Evangelism', *The Churchman Journal: An International Journal of Theology*, Vol. 95.
Gladwell, Malcolm, 2000, *The Tipping Point: How Little Things Can Make a Big Difference*, Boston, MA: Little, Brown.
Goldhill, Simon, 2016, *A Very Queer Family Indeed: Sex, Religion and the Bensons in Victorian Britain*, Chicago, IL and London: Chicago University Press.
Guder, Darrell, 2015, *Called to Witness: Doing Missional Theology*, Grand Rapids, MI: Eerdmans.
Heelas, Paul and Linda Woodhead, 2005, *The Spiritual Revolution: Why Religion is Giving Way to Spirituality*, Religion and Spirituality in the Modern World, Oxford: Blackwell.

Hiestand, Gerald and Todd Wilson, 2015, *The Pastor as Theologian: Resurrecting an Ancient Vision*, Grand Rapids, MI: Zondervan.
Holmes III, Urban T., 1982, *What is Anglicanism?*, Harrisburg, PA: Morehouse Publishing.
Ishiguro, Kazuo, 1989, *The Remains of the Day*, London: Faber and Faber.
Jaques, Elliott, 1976, *A General Theory of Bureaucracy*, London: Heinemann.
Jenkins, Philip, 2021, *Climate, Catastrophe and Faith: How Changes in Climate Drive Religious Upheaval*, Oxford: Oxford University Press.
Jones, Robert P., 2016, *The End of White Christian America*, New York: Simon & Schuster.
Jones, Robert P., 2020, *White Too Long: The Legacy of White Supremacy in American Christianity*, New York: Simon & Schuster.
Julian of Norwich, 2015, *Revelations of Divine Love*, Oxford World's Classics, trans. Barry Windeatt, Oxford: Oxford University Press.
Katz, Robert, Sarah Ogilvie, Jane Shaw and Linda Woodhead, 2021, *Gen Z Explained: The Art of Living in a Digital Age*, Chicago, IL and London: Chicago University Press.
Kimber, Jonathan, 2014, 'Ecclesiology and Leadership in the Church of England Today', PhD thesis, King's College, London.
Lemon, Bailey, 2020, 'Why this Radical Leftist is Disillusioned by Leftist Culture', *Medium Magazine*, 16 February 2020.
Lewis, C. S., 1955, *Surprised by Joy*, London: Geoffrey Bles.
Long Jr, Edward LeRoy, 2001, *Patterns of Polity*, Cleveland, OH: Pilgrim Press.
MacKinnon, D. M., 2011, *Philosophy and the Burden of Theological Honesty: A Donald MacKinnon Reader*, ed. J. C. McDowell, London: Continuum/T & T Clark.
Naim, Moisés, 2013, *The End of Power: From Boardrooms to Battlefields*, New York: Basic Books.
Newbigin, Lesslie, 1986, *Foolishness to the Greeks*, London: SPCK.
Nisbet, R. A., 1970, *The Social Bond: An Introduction to the Study of Society*, New York: Alfred A. Knopf.
O'Donohue, John, 2008, 'This is the Time to Be Slow', in *To Bless the Space Between Us: A Book of Blessings*, London: Convergent Books, Penguin Random House.
Oliver, Gordon, 2012, *Ministry Without Madness*, London: SPCK.
Percy, Emma, 2014 *Mothering as Metaphor for Ministry*, London: Routledge.
Percy, Emma, 2015, *What Clergy Do: Especially When It Looks Like Nothing*, London: SPCK.
Percy, Martyn, 1996, *Words, Wonders and Power*, London: SPCK.

REFERENCES AND FURTHER READING

Percy, Martyn, 2021, *The Humble Church: Renewing the Body of Christ*, London: Canterbury Press.

Percy, Martyn and Emma Percy (eds), 2023, *Spirit of Witness*, London: Canterbury Press.

Pytches, David and Brian Skinner, 1993, *New Wineskins: Defining New Structures for Worship and Growth Beyond Existing Parish Boundaries*, Guildford: Eagle Books.

Robinson, J. A. T., 1965, *The New Reformation*, London: SCM Press.

Shillington, V. G., 2001, 'Salt of the Earth', *The Expository Times*, Vol. 112, No. 4, January 2001, pp. 120–22.

Talent Management for Future Leaders and Leadership Development for Bishops and Deans: A New Approach, 2014, Report of the Lord Green Steering Group.

Thompson, Kenneth, 1970, *Bureaucracy and Church Reform: The Organizational Response of the Church of England to Social Change, 1880–1965*, Oxford: Oxford University Press.

Thung, Mady, 1976, *The Precarious Organization: Sociological Explorations of the Church's Mission and Structure*, The Hague: Mouton & Co.

Vanhoozer, Kevin and Owen Strachan, 2015, *The Pastor as Public Theologian: Reclaiming a Lost Vision*, Grand Rapids, MI: Baker Academic.

Vidler, Alec, 1957, *Essays in Liberality*, London: SCM Press.

Wagner, C. Peter, 1976, *Your Church Can Grow*, Glendale, CA: Regal Books.

Wagner, C. Peter, 2010, *Church Planting for a Greater Harvest*, Eugene, OR: Wipf & Stock.

Weil, Simone, 1951, *Waiting on God*, New York: Harper and Row.

Acknowledgements of Sources

The author and publisher acknowledge with thanks permission to use the following material under copyright.

Anna Blaedel, 'New Beatitudes', Enfleshed, https://enfleshed.com/. Used by permission.

Patricia Fresen, Translation of Beatitudes, adapted, https://bridgetmarys.blogspot.com/2017/02/the-beatitudes-as-translated-from.html. Used by permission.

Cartoon: 'He says there's no scientific basis for global warming'. © Clive Goddard. Used by permission of Clive Goddard.

Minnie Louise Haskins, 'The Gate of the Year', written in 1908, privately published in 1912, in a collection titled *The Desert*.

Edwin Morgan, 'Open the Doors', written for the opening of the Scottish Parliament 9 October 2004 © Scottish Parliament Corporate Body (contains information licensed under the Scottish Parliament Copyright Licence). Used by permission.

John O'Donohue, 'This is the Time to Be Slow', in *To Bless the Space Between Us: A Book of Blessings*, copyright © 2008 by John O'Donohue. Used by permission of Doubleday, an imprint of the Knopf Doubleday Publishing Group, a division of Penguin Random House LLC. All rights reserved.

Index of Names and Subjects

abiding 178–9
abundance, of God's love 199–207, 211
abuse 161–2, 186, 192–3
Adam and Eve 99
adiaphora 72
Ahmad, Asam 160–3
Aramaic xx, 51–2, 130–2
'Archdruid Eileen' 18–19
Augustine (Saint) 93
authority 37–9

balance 102–3
Ballard, J. G. 148
Barth, Karl 13
BBC 65–6, 70, 74
Beatitudes xix, 51–4, 130–4, 152–3, 154–6, 215–16
Benedict, Rule 35–6
Benson, Edward White 105, 106, 108, 126–7
Bergoglio, Jorge Mario (archbishop) 184, 186
Biggar, Nigel 168
bishops
  in the House of Lords 58–9, 85–6
  in the New Testament 108
  out of their depth 38
  Pastoral Rule for 36
  public expectations of 89–90
  styles of polity 45
  their calling 32–3, 63
  in the US Episcopalian Church 143–4
Blaedel, Anna 154–6
blessing 51–4

Canute 78, 137–8
care 43, 47
Chang, Jung 8–9, 18
China, Great Leap Forward 8–10, 17–18
Christian X (king of Denmark) 127
church
  authority of 39
  as body 35
  calling xv–xvi, 27–8, 40, 210, 214
  Christ-like 32
  as institution xix, 43
  as organization 36–7
  as public space 39
  reputational management 150
Church of England
  bishops and their ministry 57–63, 118, 123
  Clergy Discipline Measure 44–5
  corruption 187–98
  decline 77–80, 160, 163

227

diocesan structures 102–8, 117–21, 123–4
establishment 79–88
General Synod 162, 187
Governance Review Group 27–33, 40, 41–50
hypocrisy 192
irrelevance 79, 83, 88, 162
Mission Enabling Teams 82–3, 140
organizational chaos 14–15, 46–50
parishes 82–3, 105, 115, 140
safeguarding practices 29–30, 45–7, 118, 120–1, 187–98
secrecy 194
white Evangelicals 146–7
church growth 3–8, 12–20, 108
and decline 77–9
churches
authority of 37–8
not businesses 112–13
clergy *see* ordained ministry
climate change 83–4, 138–41, 148–9
contempt 72–4, 99–100
coronations 86–7
corruption, and sin 184–6
Cox, Harvey 191

Danish Lutheran church 127–8
despair 159, 171
disestablishment 84
dissent 72–3, 100, 160
Douglas-Klotz, Neil 130

Easter 183–4
ecclesiocracy 106, 121
Eileen ('Archdruid') 18–19
Episcopal Church (USA) 142–4, 169

equality 38–9, 204
eroticism 15–16
Eucharist 190
Evangelicals in the USA 144–5
evangelistic initiatives, ineffectiveness 79–80

faith, as self-defence 187
Fayol, Henri 34–5
Field, Frank 153–4
forgiveness 183–6
Francis (of Assisi) 173–4
Francis (Pope) 97, 184, 188
freedom, compared with equality 39
Fresen, Patricia 215–16

Galilee 130–1
Gen Z 124–6
Gladwell, Malcolm 72
Goldhill, Simon 126
goodness, not expecting reward 209–10
Great Leap Forward 8–10, 17–18, 20
Gregory Centre for Church Multiplication 3–6, 14
Guder, Darrell 7–8

Haidt, Jonathan 164
Hardy, Daniel Wayne 31–2, 97
Haskins, Minnie Louise 178–9
Holmes, Urban Terry III 29
hope 171–2, 177, 190, 210–11
giving up 195
house churches 4–5
House of Lords 58–9, 85–6
human rights 62
humility 98–9, 214
hypocrisy 154

impartiality xxv, 64–76

INDEX OF NAMES AND SUBJECTS

indifference 191–2
institutions 99–100
  churches as 64–76
irrationality 164–5
Ishiguro, Kazuo 170–1

Jairus 186
Jaques, Elliott 31, 36
Jenkins, Philip 148–9
Jesus
  God with us 179–80
  the language he spoke xx, 51–2, 130–2
  his ministry embodying the kingdom 13, 188
  his ministry as precarious xiv–xv
  his parables 199–206
  and parties 199–200
  and Temple money-changers 190–1
John the Baptist 54
Jones, Robert P. 142, 144, 146–8
journalism 66–74
joy 195–6
Julian of Norwich 212

kenosis 32, 214
Kimber, Jonathan 121
King, Edward 105, 106, 108
kingdom of God 153–4, 175–6, 202–5

law 197–8
leadership
  compared with management 34–6, 90–2, 107, 160
  grounded 156
  unaccountable 188
Lemon, Bailey 165–6
Lewis, C. S. 195

liberalism xxiv–xxv
Long, Edward LeRoy Jr 45
love
  God's 203–4, 210
  unconditional 214

McGavran, Donald 12–13
MacKinnon, Donald 213
management 17
  compared with leadership 34–6, 90–2, 107, 160
  functions 34–5
  not for clergy 36, 112
marriage, compared to church 109–11
maturity 131–4, 215–16
May, Rollo 14
Methodist Church, organizational structure 48–9
Modern Church xxi–xxii
Morgan, Edwin 174–5

Naim, Moisés 215
Newbigin, Lesslie 6–7
news reporting 66–74
Nolan principles 28, 193–4

O'Donohue, John 178
Oliver, Gordon 17
ordained ministry
  as an occupation 112–14
  and central management 36
  requirements for 31
  see also bishops; clergy
organizations, useful but limited 43–4
Oxford, University structure 48

parables 199–206
parties 199–200
pastoral care, for clergy 119

pastoral ministry 90, 91–3
Percy, Emma, poems by 92–3,
   129, 133, 152–3, 213
popes, and the Curia 46
populism 71
power, God's vs human
   214–15
prayer, in Aramaic 132
precariousness xiv–xvi, 101,
   210
Pytches, David 15

Rampant-Sacred-Irrationality
   165–9
religion
   decline 77–8
   as moral superiority 187–8
respair 124–5, 159, 171–3,
   177
revolutions 125–6
ripening 131–2, 215–16
risk 210
Robinson, John A. T. 106
Ruskin, John 201

safeguarding 120–1
safeguarding *see also under*
   Church of England
salt of the earth 21–4
salvation, not rationed 203–4
same-sex relationships 5, 62,
   70, 128
Savile, Jimmy 74
scandal 189
Scottish Parliament building
   174–5

Scruton, Roger 9–10
sea-level rise 138–41
self-sufficiency xix
sexual abuse 186, 191–3
sexuality 126–8
sin, and corruption 184–5
Skinner, Brian 15
slavery 169
social media 69, 208
social work 45–6
stewardship 120
stumbling-blocks 189–90, 192
systemic disorder 44–5

Thompson, Kenneth 114
Thung, Mady 36–7
Trump, Donald 10–11
truth xxiv–xxvi, 71, 74, 160,
   168
Tutu, Desmond 196

Ukraine 66–7
Underhill, Evelyn 32

values 124, 149–50
victims' groups 196
Vidler, Alec xxv

Wagner, C. Peter 12–13, 15
wealth, pointless 154
Weil, Simone xxiii
Wimber, John 15
Woodhead, Linda 121–2
Wyntoun, Andrew of 177

Yushchenko, Victor 66–7